Letters Conversations and Recollections of S. T. Coleridge

S. T. Coleridge

BIBLIOLIFE

LETTERS

CONVERSATIONS AND RECOLLECTIONS

OF

S. T. COLERIDGE.

Pliny writ his Letters for the Public; so did Seneca, so did Balzac, Voiture, &c. &c.; Tully did not: and therefore these give us more pleasure than any which have come down to us from antiquity. When we read them we pry into a secret which was intended to be kept from us. That is a pleasure. We see Cato and Brutus and Pompey and others, such as they really were, and not such as the gaping multitude of their own age took them to be, or as Historians and Poets have represented them to ours. That is another pleasure.—BOLINGBROKE TO SWIFT.

IN TWO VOLUMES.
VOL. I.

LONDON:
EDWARD MOXON, DOVER STREET.

1836.

LONDON:
BRADBURY AND EVANS, PRINTERS,
WHITEFRIARS.

TO ELIZABETH AND ROBIN,

THE FAIRY PRATTLER, AND STILL MEEK BOY OF

THE LETTERS,

AND THROUGH YOU EQUALLY TO YOUR YOUNGER BROTHERS

AND SISTERS,

THESE LETTERS AND REMINISCENCES

OF THE VERY REMARKABLE AND WONDERFUL MAN WHO

WATCHED YOUR EARLIEST DEVELOPMENT,

AND TO WHOM YOU WERE OBJECTS OF TENDEREST LOVE

AND SOLICITUDE,

ARE INSCRIBED BY YOUR

AFFECTIONATE PARENT.

PREFACE.

Having for more than sixteen years enjoyed a large share of the affectionate regards, sympathy, and inmost confidence of the most variously gifted and extraordinary man that has appeared in these latter days, it has been to me a most melancholy, though not unpleasing, task, to arrange these materials, so as to give to you, my dearest children, some idea—alas, how poor!—how inadequate it *must* be, of that friend for whose sake you are, if possible, more dear to me.

To you, my dearest Elizabeth, the fairy Prattler of the Letters, and to you, Robin, the still meek Boy, I am especially desirous to convey, through these fragments, some better, some more entirely individualised, notion of the earliest friend, best, and first lost.

Of the no less loving, not less to be loved Charles Lamb, having been house-mates, your recollections need not this aid. I stood beside the Grave, and saw when it received their loved forms, and, since then, I seem to have lived on their memories.

Lamentation and regrets for the loss of such men, would be felt by all who knew—and were worthy to be known by—them, as a grievous wrong done to their memories. If we have not learned from, and for, these men, that boisterous grief, grief of which the signs are external and visible, is an inadequate and unfitting tribute; then, as relates to the manner in which they would be remembered, they have failed to make themselves understood.

Thoughts that are indeed too deep for tears, mingle with all our recollections of that grey-haired Old Man, that mightiest Master of Poetry and of Philosophy in its truest and only valuable sense.

To have known such a man, to have shared his many sorrows and sufferings, and to have partaken of the few and far between gleams of glad and joyous sunshine which fell to his lot, are recollections to be cherished in the inner sanctuary of our hearts. Few indeed as were the gleams of genial and warm and cordial uprising of that noble and pure-minded Spirit in later years, still to him it was an ever new delight to impart, all he had learnt, all he had experienced, and much in which he could only have been his own teacher, to those who sought him in sincerity and simplicity of heart.

I seek most earnestly to make you know the minds of these, to you, Ancient of Days; and I think I shall best effect this by allowing them to speak for themselves. "Of the Dead," says the old adage, "nothing but what is good." I say to you " *nothing—or what is true.*"

Of the first of these friends, both lost in the past year, I shall chiefly speak to you; more full and sufficient records of the last I earnestly hope to see from the Pen of one every way fitted, both by love and fine appreciation of his Character, to the task.

I have given with the Letters such brief Notices and Recollections as seemed likely to enable you to appreciate that great and extraordinary mind, that greatest and truest philosopher, in the highest and only true sense of that term, in its combination with Love.

Upon the Letters and Conversations, however, I chiefly rely for conveying to you some slight image, though vastly inadequate, of the mind of this wonderful, this myriad-minded man, whose loss is however far too recent to admit of just or adequate Estimation.

Cherished and sustained by his extraordinary Intellect, and still more by the Love and Sympathy in which, like a vast reservoir, he always super-abounded, and the fulness of which seemed to arise from its overflowing, I have been able to arrive at settled and definite conclusions upon all matters to which I have heretofore attached value or interest. When I say that I have arrived at settled conclusions, you will not for a moment believe that my opinions can or *ought* to be received by others of a totally different experience, as truths for *their* minds; still less that matters which depend upon individual experience and temperament can be permanent truths for all time. You will find, and this it is which I wish to impress upon your minds, that a spirit of pure and intense *humanity*, a spirit of love and kindness, to which nothing is too large, for which nothing is too small, will be to you, as it has ever been to me, its own " exceeding great reward."

This, my dear Children, and I do not now address you only, nor your younger brothers and sisters, but I would fain speak to, and, on this point at least, could wish to be heard by, all young and confiding minds,—has been to me a solace in sorrow, an unspeakable reliance and support when all outward has been lowering and overcast. This indeed it is, in the language of an early letter, "Which, like an ample Palace, contains many mansions for every other kind of Knowledge (or renders it unnecessary); which deepens and extends the interest of every other (knowledge or faculty), gives it new charms and additional purpose: the study of which, rightly pursued, is beyond any other entertaining, beyond all others tends at once to *tranquillise* and *enliven*, to keep the mind elevated and stedfast, the Heart humble and tender." In this is the purest source of mental self-reliance, of self-dependence, and thence INDEPENDENCE, under all circumstances.

LETTERS, CONVERSATIONS,

AND

RECOLLECTIONS.

LETTER I.

Wednesday Morning, Jan. 28th, 1818.

DEAR SIR,

Your friendly letter was first delivered to me at the lecture-room door on yesterday evening, ten minutes before the lecture, and my spirits were so sadly depressed by the circumstance of my hoarseness, that I was literally incapable of reading it. I now express my acknowledgments, and with them the regret that I had not received the letter in time to have availed myself of it.

When I was young I used to laugh at flattery, as, on account of its absurdity, I now abhor it, from my repeated observations of its mischievous effects. Amongst these, not the least is, that it renders honourable natures more slow and reluctant in expressing their real feelings in praise of the deserving, than, for the interests of truth and virtue, might be desired. For the weakness of our moral and intellectual being, of which the comparatively strongest are often the most, and the most painfully, conscious, needs the confirmation derived from the coincidence and sympathy of the friend, as much as the voice of honour within us denounces the pretences of the flatterer. Be assured, then, that I write as I think, when I tell you that, from the style and thoughts of your letter, I should have drawn a very different conclusion from that which you appear to have done, concerning both your talents and the cultivation which they have received. Both the matter and manner are manly, simple, and correct.

Had I the time in my own power, compatibly with the performance of duties of immediate urgency, I would endeavour to give you, by letter, the most satisfactory answer to your questions that my reflections and the experience of my own fortunes could supply. But, at all events, I will not omit to avail myself of your judicious suggestion in my last lecture, in which it will form a consistent part of the subject and purpose of the discourse. Meantime, believe me, with great respect,

Your obliged fellow-student

of the true and the beseeming,

S. T. COLERIDGE.

The suggestion here alluded to was, if I remember rightly, as to the best mode of re-exciting that interest in and for mental cultivation and refinement, which, from lapse of time, had in most men actively employed, become dormant. This was fully treated in the last lecture.

LETTER II.

Sept. 20*th*, 1818.

DEAR SIR,

Those who have hitherto chosen to take notice of me, as known to them only by my public character, have for the greater part taken out, not, indeed, a poetical, but a critical, license to *make game* OF me, instead of sending game TO me. Thank heaven! I am in this respect more tough than tender. But, to be serious, I heartily thank you for your polite remembrance; and, though my feeble health and valetudinarian stomach force me to attach no little value to the present itself, I feel still more obliged by the kindness that prompted it.

I trust that you will not come within the purlieus of Highgate without giving me the opportunity of assuring you personally that I am, with sincere respect,

Your obliged,

S. T. COLERIDGE.

LETTER III.

Dec. 2nd, 1818.

My Dear Sir,

I cannot express how kind I felt your letter. Would to Heaven I had had many with feelings like yours, " accustomed to express themselves warmly and (as far as the word is applicable to you, even) enthusiastically." But, alas! during the prime manhood of my intellect I had nothing but cold water thrown on my efforts. I speak not now of my systematic and most unprovoked maligners. On *them* I have retorted only by pity and by prayer. These may have, and doubtless *have*, joined with the frivolity of " the reading public " in checking and almost in preventing the sale of my works; and so far have done injury to my purse. *Me* they have not injured. But I have loved with enthusiastic self-oblivion those who have been so well pleased that I should, year after year, flow with a hundred nameless rills into *their* main stream, that they could find nothing but cold praise and effective discouragement of every attempt of mine to roll onward in a distinct current of my own; who *admitted* that the Ancient Mariner, the Christabel, the Remorse, and some pages of the Friend were not without merit, but were abundantly anxious to acquit their judgments of any blindness to the very numerous defects. Yet they *knew* that to *praise*, as mere praise, I was characteristically, almost constitutionally, indifferent. In sympathy alone I found at once nourishment and stimulus; and for sympathy *alone* did my heart crave. They knew, too, how long and faithfully I had acted on the maxim, never to admit the *faults* of a work of genius to those who denied or were incapable of feeling and understanding the *beauties;* not from wilful partiality, but as well knowing that in *saying* truth I should, to such critics, convey falsehood. If, in one instance, in my literary life, I have appeared to deviate from this rule, first, it was not till the fame of the writer (which I had been for fourteen years successively toiling like a second Ali to build up) had been established; and, secondly and chiefly, with the purpose and, I may safely add, with the *effect* of rescuing the necessary task from Malignant Defamers, and in order to set forth the excellencies and the trifling proportion which the defects bore to the excellencies. But this, my dear sir, is a mistake to which affectionate natures are too liable, though I do not remember to have ever seen it noticed,—the mistaking those who are desirous and well pleased to be loved *by* you, for those who love you. Add, as a more general cause, the fact that I neither am nor ever have been of any party. What wonder, then, if I am left to decide which has been my worse enemy, the broad, pre-determined abuse of the Edinburgh Review, &c., or the cold and brief compliments, with the warm *regrets*, of the Quarterly? After all, however, I have now but one sorrow relative to the ill success of my literary toils (and toils they have been, *though not undelightful toils*), and this arises wholly from the almost insurmountable difficulties which the anxieties of to-day oppose to my completion of the great work, the form and

materials of which it has been the employment of
the best and most genial hours of the last twenty
years to mature and collect.

If I could but have a tolerably numerous audi-
ence to my first, or first and second Lectures on
the HISTORY of PHILOSOPHY, I should entertain
a strong hope of success, because I know that
these lectures will be found by far the most interesting and *entertaining* of any that I have yet
delivered, independent of the more permanent
interests of rememberable instruction. Few and
unimportant would the errors of men be, if they
did but know, first, *what they themselves meant;*
and, secondly, what the *words* mean by which they
attempt to convey their meaning; and I can conceive no subject so well fitted to exemplify the
mode and the importance of these two points as
the History of Philosophy, treated as in the scheme
of these lectures. Trusting that I shall shortly
have the pleasure of seeing you here,

I remain, my dear Sir,

Yours, most sincerely,

S. T. COLERIDGE.

This letter, as well as some more specific allusions and charges in after letters, I have thought it a sacred duty to publish; no admiration or reverence for the Great Living being for a moment to be placed against the higher duty to the greater, or, perhaps, I should say, the more greatly various, Dead. The conclusion to which I have come, from an intimate and thorough knowledge of the circumstances is, that, judged by all received rules, my much-loved friend had not *generous* usage. Far from me, however, be it to attribute blame; I am rather inclined to ascribe this seeming want of generous feeling, of sympathy, to an incompatibility of adaptation. How expressive is this passage:—" In sympathy alone I found at once nourishment and stimulus; and for sympathy *alone* did my heart crave," coupled as it is in my knowledge with the mention of his labour for fourteen years to build up the fame of his friend; and how affecting the allusion to the mistake of having supposed " those to love him who were well pleased to be loved by him."

LETTER IV.

Highgate, Sept. 30th, 1819.

MY DEAR SIR,

Returned from Ramsgate, I hasten to assure you that, next to seeing you, I have pleasure in hearing from you: and wish the former in preference, not merely from the greater mutual enjoyment, but likewise because one can convey more, and with greater assurance of being understood, in an hour, than one could write in a day. On the other hand, letters are more permanent, and an epistolary correspondence more endearing, like all marks of remembrance in absence.

My sentiments concerning the expediency, and both moral and intellectual advantages of a trade or profession, for such as fix their ultimate end on objects nobler than trades or professions can bestow on the most favoured of their followers, may be learnt from the eleventh chapter of my Literary

Life, which, though addressed to a small and particular class, yet permits a more general application. To you, my dear young friend, I should say, temptations and preventives—the poisons and the antidotes—are pretty evenly dispersed through all the different accredited paths of life. Nay, those temptations which are foreknown and foreseen as most appertinent to our particular calling, are commonly least dangerous, or even cease to be temptations to a mind forearmed by principles and aspirations like yours. The false step is more likely to take place in the recoil than the advance; in the neglect rather than in the too eager pursuit of the means; in under, rather than over, valuing the advantages of wealth and worldly respectability. The true plan on which you should regulate your conduct and feelings, (that, at least, which to me appears such) is the following. Propose to yourself from the present hour such views of action and enjoyment, as will make the leisure attached to independence, and honourably earned by previous industry, the fair object of a wise man's efforts and a good man's desires. Meantime, let the

chosen *employments* of the years in *hope* be the
relaxations of the time present, of the years devoted
to present duties, and, among these, to the means
of realising that hope ; thus you will answer two
great ends at once. Your inward trains of thought,
your faculties, and your feelings, will be preserved
in a fitness and, as it were, contempered to a life
of ease, and capable of enjoying leisure, because
both able and disposed to *employ* it. Secondly,
while you thus render future affluence more and
more desirable, you will at the same time prevent
all undue impatience, and disarm the temptation of
poisoning the allotted interval by *anxieties*, and
anxious schemes and efforts to get rich *in haste*.
There is yet one other inducement to look on your
existing appointment with complacency. Every
improvement in knowledge, and the moral power
of wielding and directing it, will *tell for more,*—have
a wider and more benignant influence,—than the
same accomplishment would in a man who belonged
to one of the learned professions. Both your information and your example will fall where they
are most wanted, like the noiseless dews in Malta,

where rain comes seldom and no regular streams are to be met with. As to your present studies, for such portions of your time as you can prudently appropriate to reading, without wrong to the claims of health and *social* relaxation, there is one department of knowledge, which, like an ample palace, contains within itself mansions for every other knowledge; which deepens and extends the interest of every other, gives it new charms and additional purpose; the study of which, rightly and *liberally* pursued, is beyond any other *entertaining*, beyond all others tends at once to tranquillize and enliven, to keep the mind elevated and steadfast, the heart humble and tender : it is *biblical theology*—the philosophy of religion, the religion of philosophy. I would that I could refer you to any *book* in which such a plan of reading had been sketched out, in detail or even but generally.

Alas ! I know of none. But most gladly will I make the attempt to supply this desideratum by conversation, and then by letter. But of this when I have next the pleasure of seeing you at Highgate.

You have perhaps heard that my publisher is a bankrupt.

* * * * *

* * * * *

* * * * * *

All the profits from the sale of my writings, which I should have had, and which, in spite of the accumulated disadvantages under which the works were published, would have been consider-able, I have lost; and not only so, but have been obliged, at a sum larger than all the profits made by my lectures, to purchase myself my own books and the half copyrights. Well, I am now *sole* proprietor, and representing my works by cyphers, and the author by I, my emblem might be 0000I. I have withdrawn them from sale. This is rather hard, but perhaps my comet may some time or other have its perihelion of popularity, and then the *tail*, you know, whisks round to the other end; and for 0000I, lo! and behold, 10,000. Mean-time, enough for me to thank God that, relatively to my fellow men at least, I have been " sinned against, not sinning ;" and relatively to my Maker, these afflictions are but penances of mercy, less than the least of my forfeitures.—I hope you will soon take pot-luck with us.

Believe me, with esteem and regard,

Yours,

S. T. Coleridge.

Leaving out the particular expression of *biblical theology*, liable to be interpreted, or, rather, misinterpreted by every believer in belief according to his own particular faith or delusion, and keeping constantly in mind what the writer intended to convey, viz. the philosophy of humanity, the humanity of philosophy, I am not aware that I can recommend to your perusal, or press earnestly and affectionately upon your attention, any letter, essay, or advice, so beautifully expressed, or, when applied to practice, so well adapted to secure that happiness which surpasseth understanding; far, very far, surpasseth adequate expression. Often do I dwell upon the recommendation, to " let the chosen *employments* of the years in hope be the

relaxations of the time present, of the years devoted
to present duties, and, among these, to the means
of realising that hope : thus you will answer two
great ends at once. Your inward trains of thought,
your faculties, and your feelings, will be preserved
in a fitness, and, as it were, contempered to a life
of ease, and capable of enjoying leisure, because
both able and disposed to *employ* it. Secondly;
while you thus render affluence *more desirable,* you
will prevent all undue impatience, and disarm the
temptation of poisoning the allotted interval by
anxieties, and anxious schemes and efforts to get
rich *in haste.*"

I would fain hope that, not only for you but for
all others, riches, *as such,* will be better appreciated
ere your career commences ; this is my anxious
hope for others—for all. For you, it shall be my
care to place before you irresistible examples and
illustrations of the frightful evils of contemplating
riches, power, fame, as *ends* to be sought and
valued for their own sake, not as *means* to greater
and higher *ends,*—the high aim and purpose of

destroying these fruitful sources of crime and misery, or of subjecting them to *general* not *individual* advancement.   Alas! could I but recal

" The time when, though my path was rough,
   The joy within me dallied with distress,
   And all misfortunes were but as the stuff
   Whence Fancy made me dreams of happiness ;
   When hope grew round me like the twining vine,
   And fruits and foliage, not my own, seemed mine:"

I might then have some hope of conveying to you with good effect the results of my experience.

" But seared thoughts now bow me down to earth,
   Nor care I that they rob me of my mirth.
   But, oh! each visitation
   Suspends what nature gave me at my birth,
   My shaping spirit of imagination.
   For not to think of what I needs must feel,
   But to be still and patient all I can,
   And haply by abstruse research to steal
   From my own nature all the natural man,—
   This is my sole resource, my only plan ;
   Till that which suits a part infects the whole,
   And now is almost grown the habit of my soul."

LETTER V.

Dec. 13*th*, 1819.

MY DEAR SIR,

Accept my affectionate thanks; and, in mine, conceive those of my housemates included. Would to heaven I had more than barren thanks to offer you. If you, or rather your residence, were nearer to me, and I could have more of your society, I should feel this the less. It was, for me at least, unfortunate, that, almost every time you have been here, I should have been engaged in the only way that I should have suffered to be a pre-engagement, viz. the duties of friendship. These are now discharged; and whenever you can give me a day, henceforward, I shall have nothing to do but to enjoy it. I could not help " winning an hour from the hard season," as Milton says, the day before yesterday, by surrendering my reason to the detail of a day-dream, as I was going over, and after I had gone over, a very pretty house, with beautiful garden and grounds, and a still more lovely prospect, at the moderate rent of 60*l*. and taxes proportionally low, discussing the question with myself, as seriously as if it were actually to be decided, how far the rising at eight, breakfasting, and riding, driving, or staging to London, and returning by the stage or otherwise, would be advantageous to your health; and then the ways and means of improving and enjoying our Sundays, &c. All I can say in excuse of these air-built castles is, that they bring with them no bills for brick and mortar, no quarrels with the masons, no indignation at the deceits and lures of the architects, surveyor, &c. when the final expense is found to treble the amount of the well-paid and costly calculation: in short, that if they do no honour to the head, they leave no harm in the heart. And then, *poeta fuimus:* and the philosopher, though pressing with the weight of an Etna, cannot prevent the poet from occasionally changing sides, and manifesting his existence by smoke traversed by electrical flashes from the crater.

Have you seen Cobbett's last number? It is the most *plausible* and the best written of any thing I have seen from *his* pen, and *apparently* written in a less fiendish spirit than the average of his weekly effusions. The self-complacency with which he assumes to himself exclusively, truths which he can call his own only as a horse-stealer can appropriate a stolen horse, by adding mutilation and deformities to robbery, is as *artful* as it is amusing. Still, however, he has given great additional publicity to weighty truths, as *ex. gr.* the hollowness of *commercial* wealth; and, from whatever dirty corner or straw moppet the ventriloquist Truth causes her words to proceed, I not only listen, but must bear witness that it is Truth talking. His conclusions, however, are palpably absurd—give to an over-peopled island the countless back settlements of America, and countless balloons to carry thither man and maid, wife and brat, beast and baggage— and then we might rationally expect that a general crash of trade, manufactures, and credit, might be as mere a summer thunderstorm in Great Britain as he represents it to be in America.

One deep, most deep, impression of melancholy, did Cobbett's letter to Lord Liverpool leave on my mind,—the conviction that, wretch as he is, he is an overmatch in intellect for those, in whose hands Providence, in its retributive justice, seems to place the destinies of our country; and who yet rise into respectability, when we compare them with their parliamentary opponents.

I am commanded to add an especial request, that it may not be long before you make yourself visible on the banks of Lake Superior.

Ever, my dear sir,

Yours faithfully and affectionately,

S. T. COLERIDGE.

The tendency of the age is now decidedly practical, and the advocates of abstractions will do well to admit the superiority of practical knowledge; and to lay claim to it as springing directly from their speculations, from their generalizations. The very opinions here said to be heretical and damnable, are now held (such is the rapid advance of public opinion) to be stale and common-place, and

have already given way to a far more searching
inquiry into the nature and uses of *all* property.
When we see a man so highly gifted, so far differ-
ing from the common sense of his contemporaries
and immediate successors, stigmatize as a wretch,
one of the most extraordinary writers of the day,
for holding opinions which those contemporaries
have for the greatest part adopted, and many gone
far beyond, we are forcibly struck with the absurdity of all ille-isms or affirmations. If we con-
fine ourselves to the expression of an opinion, or,
if more honest, we confess our ignorance of the
matter at issue, we shall be more likely to
approach true conclusions.

Neither is it the fact, that Cobbett claimed himself to be the discoverer of any or all of the principles he advanced or advocated; he combined the
scattered truths of Paine and the preceding writers
into a practical shape; and in that form he has
brought them forward *so clearly,* so often, and in
so many ways, that he has forced the attention of
his countrymen to the CAUSES of the evils by which
they are environed; so impressed with the import-

ance of those principles, that he will take no denial; but, at the sacrifice of ease, and that loved country-life, and those rural pursuits, in the midst of which he is so happy, and so fond of creating happiness, he prostrates opposition, and is determined that what he has devoted his whole life to make easy to the meanest capacity, shall not perish for want of a fair trial. That Cobbett himself commits the same injustice towards others, I well know; but this proceeds in his case from an impatience of any remedies but his own, *until his own has been tried.* To you, to whom personal controversies will, as I hope, be pitiable, if not painful, I would say, that speculation upon the cause of an evil, is, like the punishment of a crime, useless in remedying *that* crime, and is only useful, *if useful at all*, in preventing *future* crimes or evils. The direction of *existing* powers and combinations, and the formation of new combinations, upon scientific and practical principles, are the matters of most importance at this time; and the knowledge necessary to the attainment and application of these principles, does not to me appear likely to be attained whilst men are in a state of social warfare; whilst the immediate or apparent interests of one man are constantly opposed to those of another, and *both*, impediments to the well-being of the whole.

LETTER VI.

20th March, 1820.

My dear Sir,

You must have thought it strange that I had taken no notice of so kind a letter from you; but the truth is, I received the little packet supposing it to contain the Cobbett only, put it in my pocket for my reading at a leisure hour, and had not opened it until the day before I last saw you. Within a few days, I hope to lay myself open to you in an express letter; till when, I can only say, that the affectionate interest you have taken in my well-being, has been not only a comfort but a spur, when I needed both, and was almost yielding at times to the apprehension, that I had sacrificed all that the world holds precious, without being able to do any effective good in a higher and nobler kind. I have sent the three volumes of the Friend, with my MS. corrections, and additions. The largest, that towards the end of the last *philosophical* essay in the third volume, had a two-fold object—to guard my own character from the suspicion of pantheistic opinions, or Spinosism (it *was* written, though not so much at large, before the work was printed, and omitted by wilfulness, or such carelessness as does not fall far short of it); and next, to impress, as far as I could, the conviction that true philosophy, so far from having any tendency to unsettle the *principles* of faith, that may and ought to be common to all men, does itself actually require them as its premises; nay, that it supposes them as its ground* —I was highly gratified to hear, and from such a man too as Mr. John Hookham Frere, that a man of rank, and of a highly cultivated mind, who had become reluctantly a sceptic, or something more, respecting

* Though myself opposed to apologetic prefaces or modifications of opinion to suit conventional influences, I give this note as an act of justice to its author.

the Christian Religion, wholly in consequence of studying Leland, Lardner, Watson, Paley, and other defenders of the Gospel on the strength of the *external* evidences—not of Christianity, but of the miracles with which its first preaching was accompanied—and of having been taught to regard the arguments, and mode of proof adopted in the works above mentioned, as the only rational ones, had read the Friend with great attention, and when he came to the passage in which I had explained the nature of miracles, their necessary dependance on a credible religion for their own credibility, &c., dropped the book (as he himself informed Mr. Frere), and exclaimed, "Thank God! I can still believe in the Gospel—I can yet be a Christian." The remark that a miracle, divested of all connection with a doctrine, is identical with witchcraft, which in all ages has been regarded with instinctive horror by the human mind, and the reference to our Lord's own declarations concerning miracles, were among the passages that particularly impressed his mind.

I should have sent a corrected copy of the

Sibylline Leaves; but for a two-legged little *accident* having torn out two leaves at the beginning, and I will no longer delay this parcel, but will transcribe at another time what I had written in them, and I hope it will not be long before you let us see you. The people here are occupied in raising and distributing relief for the poor of the hamlet. On the first day there were seven hundred and fifty applicants to whom small sums were given! It would be most un-christian moroseness not to feel delight in the unwearied zeal with which every mode and direction of charity is supported; and I hope that this is a sunshiny spot in our national character, and that this virtue will suspend the judgments that threaten the land. But it would, on the other hand, be wilful blindness not to see that the lower orders become more and more improvident in consequence, more and more exchange the sentiments of Englishmen for the feelings of Lazzaroni.

God bless you, and

S. T. Coleridge.

P.S.—Charles and Mary Lamb dined with us on Sunday.

When I next see you, that excellent brother and sister will supply me with half an hour's interesting conversation. When you know the *whole* of him, you will love him in spite of all oddities and even faults—nay, I had almost said, *for* them—*at least*, admire that under his visitations they were so few and of so little importance. Thank God, his circumstances are comfortable; and so they ought, for he has been in the India House since his fourteenth year.

I have subjoined the MS. addition mentioned above, and should wish you to read it with great care and attention in its proper place; which is, after the word 'vacuum,' in page 263, vol. iii. of the 'Friend.'

If we thoughtfully review the course of argument pursued, we shall rest in the following as our sum and ultimatum. The dialectic intellect, by exertion of its own powers exclusively, may enable us to affirm the reality of an absolute Being, generally. But here it stops. It can command neither insight nor conviction concerning the existence (or even the possibility) of the world as distinct and different from Deity. It finds itself constrained to confound the Creator with the creation; and then, cutting the knot it cannot solve, merges the latter in the former, and denies reality to all finite existence. But here the philosophizer is condemned to meet with his sure confutation in his own secret dissatisfaction, and is forced at length to shelter himself from his own importunate queries in the wretched evasion, that of Nothings no solution can be required. Wretched indeed, and weak as desperate! Nature herself—his own inevitable Nature—through every organ of sense, compels his own abused reason to reiterate the demand: How and whence did this sterile Nothing split or multiply into *plurality?* Whence this portentous transnihilation of Nothing into Nothings? What, above all, is that inward mirror, the human mind, in and for which these Nothings possess at least a relative existence? Or dost thou wait till, with a more bitter irony, Pain and Anguish and Remorse ask thee, Are WE too Nothings?

O youthful reader! (for such The Friend dares anticipate), thou, that in my mind's eye, standest beside me, like my own youth! Fresh and keen as the morning Hunter in the pursuit of Truth, glad and restless in the feeling of mental growth! O learn early, that if the Head be the Light of the Heart, the Heart is the Life of the Head : yea, that Consciousness itself, that Consciousness of which all reasoning is the varied modification, is but the Reflex of the Conscience when most luminous ; and too often a fatuous vapour, a warmthless bewildering mockery of Light, exhaled from its corruption or stagnation. Mark the inevitable result of all *consequent* reasoning, when the intellect refuses to acknowledge a higher and deeper ground than itself can supply, and weens to possess within itself the centre of its own system ! From Zeno the Eleatrice to Spinoza, and from Spinoza to Schelling, Oken, and the German " *Natur-philosophen* " of the present day, the Result has been, and ever must be, PANTHEISM, under some one or other of its modes or disguises : and it is of awful importance to the speculative Inquirer to be aware, that the seemliest of these modes differs from the most repulsive, not in its consequences, which in all alike are Atheistic, but only as far as it evinces the efforts of the individual to hide these consequences from his own consciousness.

This, then, I again repeat, is our ultimate conclusion. All *speculative* disquisition must begin with *Postulates*, authorised and substantiated by the conscience exclusively. From whatever point the reason may start, whether from the *Things that are seen* to the One Invisible, or from the idea of the ABSOLUTE ONE to the *things that are seen*, it will in either case find a chasm, which the moral being, the *spirit* and the *religion* of man, can alone fill up or overbridge. "THE LIFE IS THE LIGHT OF MAN:" and "WE LIVE BY FAITH."

I may as well state here that the writer, possessing confessedly great and extraordinary powers, has been wholly and entirely misconceived, and by none more so than those who fondly deemed him of *their* belief. *His belief* was so capacious that it contained not only theirs and a hundred others, but also their opposites, and existed in the equipoise or equilibrium. Thus, in speaking as was his wont, of Peter, towards whom he felt an especial distaste, he was accustomed to refer to the passage in Matthew, ch. xix. ver. 27, where the Janitor asks, " Behold, we have forsaken all, and followed thee ; what shall we have therefore ? " and in a humourous strain of contemptuous remark, exhibit the selfishness of the (in mind) vulgar fisherman who, having left a wretched and precarious calling, seeks to make of this a merit, and to demand a reward for that which could only be a merit, as it did not seek to obtain any earthly reward or advantage. It ought to be known that many men in these latter days, many even from the especial land of cant and *notions* used to seek to pick up the crumbs from his mental banquets; and, as these were chiefly weak-minded and superstitious men, with a few men of strong heads and minim hearts, which latter class are *not*, however, *self-deceived,* he was led, being then feeble in health, to assent to their conclusions, seeing that between minds like theirs and his giant intellect an impassable chasm existed; in short, for peace' sake he humoured them, and for sympathy, as he used to say of Cromwell, spoke in the language but not in the sense of the canters.

Charles and Mary Lamb! what recollections, pleasant and painful, do these twin names recal. Well do I remember the first time I met this most delightful couple, and the kindness with which I was received and greeted by this twin union in partition; now, alas! for a short time separated. No man that I have ever known was so well fitted to attract and engage the sympathies, the love, the affectionate regards, and the respect of ingenuous

natures. To all others his heart was (I will not
say closed) unresponsive. To you, my dear children, who from your earliest years have been
familiar with his incomings, the impression made
by the remarkable appearance of this *model-man,*
his kindness, his expressive and pensive face and
figure, must, and ever will remain; would that I
could even faintly shadow out the more admirable
qualities of his mind. Utterly unlike any or all of
his contemporaries, having had his lot cast in hard
places, he yet by a sweetness, an uncomplaining-
ness the very opposite, however, of torpid sorrow
or resignation, had fashioned for himself a happiness, a well-being peculiarly his own. To a sound
mind in a sound body, if we take sound to mean
robust, my kind and gentle-hearted friend had no
claim; but out of his very infirmities had he made
delights for himself and for all those who had the
unspeakable privilege of his intimacy. When I
think of this loved and loveable being, and of all he
has been to me, I am almost tempted to repine at
that inevitable destiny by which our being is borne
onwards; an absurdity than which nothing can be

more deplorable, if indeed *that* were not *necessary.* Often as the recollection of that familiar face flits across my memory, and the consciousness that I cannot, as heretofore, meet him in his old haunts, or see him walk in as was his wont frequently, I am tempted to repeat his own lines.

> " A month or more hath he been dead,
>   Yet cannot I by force be led
>   To think on him and the wormy bed
>   Together.

> " My sprightly neighbour, gone before
>   To that unknown and silent shore ;
>   Shall we not meet as heretofore
>   Some summer morning ? "

What a beautiful thing is faith, if it would but last for ever.

The following lines from a short poem in the Sibylline Leaves, will more vividly impress you, if you should ever be able to catch the particular, the very peculiar cadence or rhythm, which of right belongs to the poetry of Coleridge in somewhat the

same relation as a tune to a song, and without
which it would not be a song.

————" Yes! they wander on
In gladness all; but thou, methinks, most glad,
My gentle hearted Charles! for thou hast pined
And hungered after Nature many a year,
In the great city pent, winning thy way
With sad yet patient soul, through evil and pain
And strange calamity . . . Henceforth I shall know
That Nature ne'er deserts the wise and pure,
No plot so narrow, be but Nature there,
No waste so vacant, but may well employ
Each faculty of sense, and keep the heart
Awake to Love and Beauty! *and sometimes*
'Tis well to be bereft of promised good,
That we may lift the soul and contemplate
With lively joy, the joys we cannot share.
My gentle hearted Charles! when the last rook
Beat its straight path along the dusky air
Homewards, I blest it! deeming, its black wing
(Now a dim speck, now vanishing in light)
Had crossed the mighty orb's dilated glory,
While thou stoodst gazing; or, when all was still,
Flew creaking o'er thy head, *and had a charm*
For thee, my gentle hearted Charles, *to whom*
No sound is dissonant that tells of life."

I have said that I never knew any one who at all approached or resembled our delightful housemate. I am wrong; I once met a man with his smile,— HIS smile. There is nothing like it upon earth; unless, perchance, this man survives. And yet how unlike in every other regard personal and mental; not that the man, who had by some most extraordinary means acquired or appropriated this *sunshine of the face*, was at all deficient in mental qualities. He seemed amiable, thoughtful, and introspective; a man better than his condition, or rather, his calling. He was, I believe, a stock-broker, and had been with his son to traverse the haunts of his childhood, near Lymington; *with his son*, afflicted with a sudden and complete deafness; hence, perchance, these sweet smiles springing from, and compounded of, love and pain. Yet this man had never known Lamb; still his smile was the same —the *self*-same expression on a different face,—if, indeed, whilst that smile passed over it you could see any difference. I mentioned this strange encounter to Coleridge, and he immediately constructed a most delightful theory of association, and corroborated it with so many instances, that he must have been sceptical that could *at the moment* have refused him credence. To those who wish to see the only thing left on earth, *if it is still left*, of Lamb, his best and most beautiful remain,—his smile, I will indicate its possessor,—Mr. Harman, of Throgmorton Street.

Subjoined is a tribute of love and admiration from one least fitted by genius and intellectual sympathies to appreciate the loved being so much deplored. If to this disciple of the useful and the prudent Lamb appeared so worthy of homage, judge you what he was to me, and to a herd, each more worthy than I. If by a Scotchman, with whom as a nation and as individuals he acknowledged no sympathy, he was esteemed and reverenced, think what must be the loss to those better fitted, by position and by sympathy, to *relish* and enter into his opinions and pursuits. Contrast this tribute, forced as it were, from strange lips, with the reminiscences of one on whom all his kindness and self-devotion were lavished, and upon whom his charities both of mind and purse were poured out even to self-sacrifice, and then bear in mind that gratitude is a feeble flame, which needs constantly to be kept alive by a repetition of benefits, or that IN IMPROVIDENT NATURES it gives place to rancourous disparagement, even after death.

" One of the conductors of this journal did justice to a long-cherished and deeply-rooted admiration of this writer, by making a kind of pilgrimage to his house at Edmonton, where a letter from a mutual friend introduced him to the presence of one whom he would willingly have gone ten times farther to see. All stranger as he was, he had the gratification of experiencing a share—and he thought it a large one—of that kindness which Mr. Lamb had in store for all his fellow-creatures; and, after an hour's conversation, parted with the object of his journey near the famed ' Bell,' carrying with him *a profound sense of the excellence of one of the finest model-beings whom it ever was his fortune to meet.*"—*Chambers' Journal.*

LETTER VII.

Highgate, April 10*th*, 1820.

MY DEAR FRIEND,

May I venture to obtrude on you what I cannot intrust to a messenger, much less to the post. Sackville-street is not I hope more than fifteen or twenty minutes' walk from your house. It is to inquire if Mr. Caldwell is *in town*; if he be, then to leave the letter, and that is all; but if not, to learn whether he is at his living, and if so, then to transfer his present address to the letter, and put it into the nearest General Post Office box. It is of serious importance to Derwent that the inclosed should reach Mr. Caldwell with as little delay as possible, or I need not say that I should not have taxed your time and kindness merely to make a letter-carrier of you.

On Saturday evening I received a note from Mathews, which I have inclosed. I took it very

kind of him; but to obtrude myself on Walter
Scott, *nolentem volentem,* and within a furlong of
my own abode, as he knows (for Mr. Frere told
him my address), was a liberty I had no right to
take; and though it would have highly gratified
me to have conversed with a brother-bard, and to
have renewed on the mental retina the image of,
perhaps, the most extraordinary man, assuredly
the most *extraordinary* writer, of his age, yet I
dared not purchase the gratification at so high a
price as that of risking the respect which I trust
has not hitherto been forfeited by,

My dear friend,

Your obliged and very affectionate friend,

S. T. COLERIDGE.

P.S. I had not the least expectation, yet I could
not suppress a sort of fluttering hope, that my
letter might have reached you on Saturday night,
and that you might be disengaged and turn your
walk Highgate-ward. You will be delighted with
the affectionate attachment of the two brothers to
each other, the boyish high spirits with manly inde-

pendence of intellect, and, in one word, with the simplicity which is their nature, and the common *ground* on which the differences of their mind and characters (for no two can be more distinct) shoot and play. When I say that nothing can exceed their fondness for their father, I need not add that they are impatient to be introduced to you. And I can offer no better testimony of the rank you hold in my bosom, my dear . . . , than the gladness with which I anticipate their becoming your *friends,* in the noblest sense of the word. Would to Heaven their dear sister were with us, the cup of paternal joy would be full to the brim ! The rapture with which both Hartley and Derwent talk of her, quite affects Mrs. Gilman, who has always felt with a sort of lofty yet refined enthusiasm respecting the relations of an only sister to her brothers. Of all women I ever knew, Mrs. G. is the woman who seems to have been framed by Nature for a heroine in that rare species of love which subsists in a tri-unity of the heart, the moral sense, and the faculty, corresponding to what Spurzheim calls the organ of *ideality.* What in other women is *refinement* exists in her as by implication, and, *à fortiori*, in a native *fineness* of character. She often represents to my mind the best parts of the Spanish Santa Teresa, ladyhood of nature.

Vexation! and Mrs. Gillman has this moment burnt Mathews' note. The purport, however, was as follows:—" I have just received a note from Terry, informing me that Sir Walter Scott will call upon me to-morrow morning (*i. e.* Sunday) at half-past eleven. Will you contrive to be here at the same time? Perhaps the promise of your company may induce Sir Walter to appoint a day on which he will dine with me before he returns to the north."

Now as Scott had asked Terry for my address on his first arrival in town, it is not *impossible*, though not very probable, that Terry may have said,—" You will meet Coleridge at Mathews's," though I was not entitled to presume this. The bottom of all this, my dear friend, is neither more nor less than as follows:—I seem to feel that I *ought* to feel more desire to see an extraordinary man than I really do feel; and I do not wish to appear to two or three persons (as the Mr. Freres, William Rose, &c.), as if I cherished any dislike to Scott respecting the *Christabel*, and generally an increasing dislike to appear out of the common and natural mode of thinking and acting. All this is, I own, sad weakness, but I am weary of *dyspathy*.

In this last sentence may be read the whole secret of the writer's latter days. In thought, action, opinion, he always sought for harmony and agreement, and frequently created a harmony of his own. Hence his dislike of, and distaste for, the new sciences, *so called*, of Political Economy and the Utilitarian Philosophy, in which nothing is proved, nothing settled, and with respect to the very elements of which no two professors are agreed. When one of the self-sufficient of this last class, now so numerous as to infest, beset, and defile all places of public resort where anything is to be obtained, was controverting one of the more profound opinions of Coleridge, upon which he had brought to bear, *but not exhausted*, all the

stores of a mind perfectly unequalled, both with
respect to the mass of knowledge,—nay more,
true wisdom,—and the eloquence with which that
knowledge was adorned, and asserting, in opposition to views, to the comprehension of the least of
which his mechanical mind was unequal, that the
tendency of public opinion and the state of things
was in another direction, Coleridge, taking up
the down of a thistle which lay by the road
side, and holding it up, said, after observing the
direction in which it was born by the wind,—
" The tendency of that thistle is towards China,
but I know with assured certainty that it will
never get there ; nay, that it is more than probable that, after sundry eddyings and gyrations
up and down, backwards and forwards, that it will
be found somewhere near the place in which it
grew." Then, turning to me,—" I refer to your
experience, if you ever knew the probabilities, the
suppositions of any man or set of men, realised in
their main features, *permanently*. No! no! Hence,
such institutions as poor laws have never answered,
never can answer, unless the framers could compel
society to remain in the same state as when these

laws or regulations were made, which is a manifest absurdity. It was not the barbarism of our forefathers, as is so complacently taken for granted, but the flux and change of events which unfit *all laws* for after-times. Bishop Berkely, in his imaginary travels, shows very ingeniously the evil of all laws; and I have no doubt that the time will arrive when all penal laws will be held to be barbarous, and proofs of the barbarism of this and all antecedent ages."

LETTER VIII.

Saturday, April 8th, 1820, Highgate.

MY DEAR FRIEND,

It is not the least advantage of friendship, that by communicating our thoughts to another, we render them distinct to themselves, and reduce the subjects of our sorrow and anxiety to their just magnitude for our own contemplation.

As long as we inly brood over a misfortune

(there being no divisions or separate circumscriptions in things of mind, no *proper* beginning nor ending to any thought, on the one hand; and, on the other, the confluence of our recollections being determined far more by sameness or similarity of the feelings that had been produced by them, than by any positive resemblance or connection between the things themselves that are thus recalled to our attention) we establish a centre, as it were, a sort of nucleus in the reservoir of the soul; and toward this, needle shoots after needle, cluster points on cluster points, from all parts of contained fluid, and in all directions, till the mind with its best faculties is locked up in one ungenial frost. I cannot adequately express the state of feeling in which I wrote my last letter; the letter itself, I doubt not, bore evidence of its *nest* and mode of incubation, as certain birds and lizards drag along with them part of the egg-shells from which they had forced their way. Still one good end was answered. I had made a clearance, so far as to have my head in light and my eyes open; and your answer, every way worthy of you, has removed the rest.

But before I enter on this subject, permit me to refer to some points of *comparative* indifference, lest I should forget them altogether. I occasioned you to misconceive me respecting Sir Walter Scott. My purpose was to bring proofs of the energetic or inenergetic state of the minds of men, induced by the excess and unintermitted action of stimulating events and circumstances, — revolutions, battles, *newspapers*, mobs, sedition and treason trials, public harangues, meetings, dinners; the necessity in every individual of ever increasing activity and anxiety in the improvement of his estate, trade, &c., in proportion to the decrease of the actual value of money, to the multiplication of competitors, and to the almost compulsory expedience of expense, and prominence, even as the means of obtaining or retaining competence; the consequent craving after amusement as proper *relaxation*, as *rest* freed from the tedium of vacancy; and, again, after such knowledge and such acquirements as are *ready coin*, that will pass *at once*, unweighed and unassayed; to the unexampled facilities afforded for this end by reviews, magazines, &c., &c. The

theatres, to which few go to see *a play*, but to see
Master Betty or Mr. Kean, or some one individual
in some *one* part: and the single fact that our
neighbour, Mathews, has taken more, night after
night, than both the regular theatres conjointly,
and when the best comedies or whole plays have
been acted at each house, and those by excellent
comedians, would have yielded a striking instance,
and illustration of my position. But I chose an
example in literature, as more in point for the subject of my particular remarks, and because every
man of genius, who is born for his age, and capable
of acting *immediately* and widely on that age, must
of necessity *reflect* the age in the first instance,
though as far as he is a man of genius, he will
doubtless be himself reflected by it reciprocally.
Now I selected Scott for the very reason, that I do
hold him for a man of *very extraordinary* powers;
and when I say that I have read the far greater
part of his novels twice, and several three times
over, with undiminished pleasure and interest; and
that, in my reprobation of the Bride of Lammermoor (with the exception, however, of the almost

Shakspearian old witch-wives at the funeral) and of the Ivanhoe, I meant to imply the grounds of my admiration of the others, and the permanent nature of the interest which they excite. In a word, I am far from thinking that Old Mortality or Guy Mannering would have been less admired in the age of Sterne, Fielding, and Richardson, than they are in the present times; but only that Sterne, &c., would not have had the same *immediate* popularity in the present day as in their own less stimulated and, therefore, less languid reading world.

Of Sir Walter Scott's poems I cannot speak so highly, still less of the Poetry in his Poems; though even in these the power of presenting the most numerous figures, and figures with the most complex movements, and under rapid succession, in *true picturesque unity*, attests true and peculiar genius. You cannot imagine with how much pain I used, many years ago, to hear —————'s contemptuous assertions respecting Scott; and, if I mistake not, I have yet the fragments of the rough draught of a letter written by me so long

ago as my first lectures at the London Philosophical Society, Fetter Lane, and on the backs of
the unused admission tickets.

One more remark. My criticism was *confined*
to the one point of the higher degree of intellectual
activity implied in the reading and admiration of
Fielding, Richardson, and Sterne;—in moral, or, if
that be too high and inwardly a word, in *mannerly*
manliness of taste the present age and its *best*
writers have the decided advantage, and I sincerely
trust that Walter Scott's readers would be as little
disposed to relish the stupid lechery of the court-
ship of Widow Wadman, as Scott himself would
be capable of presenting it. Add, that though I
cannot pretend to have found in any of these
novels a character that even approaches in genius,
in truth of conception, or boldness and freshness of
execution to Parson Adams, Blifil, Strap, Lieute-
nant Bowling, Mr. Shandy, Uncle Toby and Trim,
and Lovelace; and though Scott's *female* characters
will not, even the very best, bear a comparison
with Miss Byron, Clementina, Emily, in Sir
Charles Grandison; nor the comic ones with

Tabitha Bramble, or with Betty (in Mrs. Bennet's Beggar Girl); and though, by the use of the Scotch dialect, by Ossianic mock-highland motley-heroic, and by extracts from the printed sermons, memoirs, &c., of the fanatic preachers, there is a good deal of *false effect* and stage trick : still the number of characters *so good* produced by one man, and in so rapid a succession, must ever remain an illustrious phenomenon in literature, after all the subtractions for those borrowed from English and German sources, or compounded by blending two or three of the old drama into one— *ex. gr.* the Caleb in the Bride of Lammermoor.

Scott's great merit, and, at the same time, his *felicity,* and the true solution of the long-sustained *interest* novel after novel excited, lie in the nature of the subject; not merely, or even chiefly, because the struggle between the Stuarts and the Presby-terians and sectaries, is still in lively memory, and the passions of the adherency to the former, if not the adherency itself, extant in our own fathers' or grandfathers' times; nor yet (though this is of great weight) because the language, manners, &c.,

introduced are sufficiently different from our own
for *poignancy*, and yet sufficiently near and similar
for sympathy; nor yet because, for the same reason, the author, speaking, reflecting, and descant-
ing in his own person, remains still (to adopt a
painter's phrase) in sufficient *keeping* with his subject matter, while his characters can both talk and
feel interestingly to *us* as men, without recourse to
antiquarian interest, and nevertheless without moral
anachronism (in all which points the Ivanhoe is so
wofully the contrary, for what Englishman cares
for Saxon or Norman, both brutal invaders, more
than for Chinese and Cochin Chinese?)—yet great
as all these causes are, the essential wisdom and
happiness of the subject consists in this,—that the
contest between the loyalists and their opponents
can never be *obsolete*, for it is the contest between
the two great moving principles of social humanity;
religious adherence to the past and the ancient, the
desire and the admiration of permanence, on the
one hand; and the passion for increase of knowledge, for truth, as the offspring of reason—in
short, the mighty instincts of *progression* and *free*

agency, on the other.　In all subjects of deep and lasting interest, you will detect a struggle between two opposites, two polar forces, both of which are alike necessary to our human well-being, and necessary each to the continued existence of the other.　Well, therefore, may we contemplate with intense feelings those whirlwinds which are for free agents the appointed means, and the only possible condition of that equilibrium in which our moral Being subsists; while the disturbance of the same constitutes our sense of life.　Thus in the ancient Tragedy, the lofty struggle between irresistible fate and unconquerable free will, which finds its equilibrium in the Providence and the future retribution of Christianity.　If, instead of a contest between Saxons and Normans, or the Fantees and Ashantees, — a mere contest of indifferents! of minim surges in a boiling fish-kettle, — Walter Scott had taken the struggle between the men of arts and the men of arms in the time of Becket, and made us feel how much to claim our well-wishing there was in the cause and character of the priestly and papal party, no less than in those of Henry and his knights, he would have opened a new mine, instead of translating into Leadenhall Street Minerva Library sentences, a cento of the most common incidents of the stately self-congruous romances of D'Urfe, Scuderi, &c. N.B. I have not read the Monastery, but I suspect that the thought or element of the faery work is from the German. I perceive from that passage in the Old Mortality, where Morton is discovered by old Alice in consequence of calling his dog Elphin, that Walter Scott has been reading Tieck's Phantasies (a collection of faery or witch tales), from which both the incident and name is borrowed.

I forget whether I ever mentioned to you, that some eighteen months ago I had planned and half collected, half manufactured and invented a work, to be entitled *The Weather-*BOUND *Traveller;* or, Histories, Lays, Legends, Incidents, Anecdotes, and Remarks, contributed during a detention in one of the Hebrides, recorded by their Secretary, Lory Mc Haroldson, Senachy in the Isle of ——.

The principle of the work I had thus expressed in the first chapter:—" Though not *fact,* must it needs be false? These things have a truth of their own, if we but knew how to look for it. There is a *humanity* (meaning by this word whatever contradistinguishes man), there is a humanity common to all periods of life, which each *period* from childhood has its own way of representing. Hence, in whatever laid firm hold of us in early life, there lurks an interest and a charm for our maturest years, but which *he* will never draw forth, who, content with mimicking the unessential, though natural defects of thought and expression, has not the skill to remove the *childish*, yet leave the *childlike* untouched. Let each of us then relate that which has left the deepest impression on his mind, at whatever period of his life he may have seen, heard, or read it; but let him tell it in accordance with the *present state* of his intellect and feelings, even as he has, perhaps (Alnaschar-like), acted it over again by the parlour fire-side of a rustic inn, with the fire and the candles for his only companions."

On the hope of my Lectures answering, I had intended to have done this work out of hand, dedicating the most genial hours to the completion of Christabel, in the belief that in the former I should be rekindling the feeling, and recalling the state of mind, suitable to the latter.—But the Hope was vain.

In stating the names and probable size of my works, I by no means meant any reference to the mode of their publication; I merely wished to communicate to you the amount of my labours. In two moderate volumes it was my intention to comprise all those more prominent and systematic parts of my lucubrations on Shakspeare as should be published (in the first instance at least, in the form of books), and having selected and arranged them, to send the more particular illustrations and analysis to some respectable magazine. In like manner, I proposed to include the philosophical critiques on Dante, Milton, Cervantes, &c. in a series of Letters entitled The Reviewer in Exile, or Critic confined to an Old Library. Provided the truths (which are, I dare affirm, original, and all tending to the same principles, and proving the endless fertility of true principle, and the decision and power of growth which it communicates to all the faculties of the mind) are but in existence, and to be read by such as might wish to read, I have no choice as to the mode; nay, I should prefer that mode which most multiplied the chances.—So too as to the order.—For *many* reasons, it had been my wish to commence with the Theological Letters: one, and not the least, is the strong desire I have to put you and Hartley and Derwent Coleridge in full possession of my whole Christian creed, with the grounds of reason and authority on which it rests; but especially to unfold the true " glorious liberty of the Gospel," by showing the distinction between doctrinal faith and its sources and historical belief, with their reciprocal action on each other; and thus, on the one hand, to do away the servile superstition which makes men *Biblio-lators*, and yet hides from them the proper excellencies, the one continued revelation of the Bible documents, which they idolise; and, on the other hand, to expose, in its native worthlessness, the so-called evidences of Christianity first brought into *toleration* by Arminius, and into fashion by

Grotius and the Socinian divines: for as such I consider all those who preach and teach in the spirit of Socinianism, though even in the outward form of a defence of the thirty-nine articles.

I have been interrupted by the arrival of my sons, Hartley and Derwent, the latter of whom I had not seen for so dreary a time. I promise myself great pleasure in introducing him to you. Hartley you have already met. Indeed, I am so desirous of this, that I will defer what I have to add, that I may put this letter in the post, time enough for you to receive it this evening; saying only, that it was not my purpose to have had any further communication on the subject but with Mr. Frere, and with him only, as a counsellor. Let me see you as soon as you can, and as often. I shall be better able hereafter to talk with you than to write to you on the contents of your last.

Your very affectionate friend,

S. T. COLERIDGE.

If it had been possible for the writer of *this* letter to have been both oracle and priest (or rather popular expounder), then indeed should we have wanted little (for the present time at least) in the way of aids to knowledge in its highest aim and tendency. But powers like his have never yet existed in conjunction with familiar and popular elucidation. There was nothing shapeless and unmeaning in anything he ever said or wrote. There were no crudities, no *easy* reading in his productions. To follow the train of his reasoning demanded *at first* severe and continued attention; and to this how few of the self-called seekers after that knowledge which is truth are equal. To him, details were of little value, except as far as they illustrated, proved, a principle; whilst to the greater part of those who latterly became his hearers, they constituted the only part of his conversation which was intelligible or of the least interest. Would that it were possible to recal some of those delightful tales which my friend used to relate in his inimitable manner, as forming part of the collection existing in his mind of the

" Weather-bound Traveller." Myself a proficient when a youth as a *raconteur*, I was still surprised at the extraordinary ease with which he produced story after story, each more incredible, more mystic, and more abounding with materials for future meditation, than the one preceding. Ardently do I hope that the fragments above alluded to have been saved, and that the worthy and excellent friend to whom they are confided will give them to the world as he finds them.

The allusion to the Socinians may need some explanation. Having for a short time, in early youth, been a convert to what is now called Unitarianism, through the instrumentality of a Mr. Friend of Cambridge (no friend to him), he had opportunities of free and unrestrained intercourse and intercommunion with the more influential and distinguished of this sect; and the result was a conviction of the insincerity (conscious or otherwise), selfishness, or, as he expressed it, self-centering, and want of moral courage, produced by this faith, or, as he again termed it, this want of faith. That this was the fact at that time, I am willing to admit; but my own experience, my own *knowledge,* of many who delight in, or *endure* this name, leads me to the conclusion, that a change has come over their spirit. To the charge of want of moral courage they appear as obnoxious now as at any previous period: nay, more—for in the earlier period of their history, the very expression of *these* opinions was an act of great moral daring; whilst at this time, when toleration is universal, it would be more in unison with that universal progression which we see in every other sect and party, to find them casting away the small remnant of superstition which they have hitherto retained, out of consideration, as it should seem, to the fouler superstitions and mental degradation by which they are still surrounded.

But my excellent friend had another cause of quarrel with this sect. He saw with what readiness they received and adopted the atrocious, the, *in any, in every* sense, hateful opinions and views of Malthus and the so called economists; a sect and a class having about as much title to that name (as first generally given to Turgot and his associates), as a crab to an apple, or a mule to a race-horse. This he attributed to the selfish and cold character of minds in which neither imagination nor love had a place, and to the restlessness superinduced by the absence of those two faculties. To observations as to their being the slaves of the circumstances by which they were surrounded, or to the education which they had received, he opposed the fact, that they were all to a great degree sceptical, and not therefore passive, recipients of *any* faith.

I have thought it fitting and desirable thus to notice, in passing, his great dislike to this class, that it may lead to a more full and satisfactory elucidation from the pen of his friend and biographer. For myself, opposed as I am both from principle and feeling to the plans and practices which this class encourages and abets,—a system at once petty in its details and mighty in the extent of its application, that tends to a tyranny, compared with which the cruelties of a Nero and a Caligula were mild and beneficent,—I am desirous and anxious to do justice to individuals who adhere from habit to this sect, and who thus share in the odium so justly incurred by the more restless, and unhappy because restless, of this party. To you especially, my dear children, and to the ingenuous youth of this age (if, perchance, this mechanical and utilitarian age should permit of ingenuous youth), there can be no need to teach or preach toleration. If it were necessary to enforce the great truth, that opinion is always the result of previous circumstances and influences, not the consequence of any choice or will of the individual mind, I should be able with ease to prove the *necessity* of charity; but this has been made so manifest, that I shall content myself with giving in this place a short extract from the " Friend " in relation to this *great truth.*

" For a subdued sobriety of temper, a practical faith in the doctrine of philosophical necessity seems the *only* preparative. That vice is the effect of error and the offspring of surrounding circumstances, the object therefore of condolence, not of anger, is a proposition easily understood and as easily demonstrated. But to make it spread from the *understanding* to the *affections,* to call it into action, not only in the great exertions of patriotism, but in the daily and hourly occurrences of social life, requires the most watchful attentions of the most energetic mind.

" It is not enough that we have once swallowed these truths; we must feed on them, as insects on a leaf, till the whole heart be coloured by their qualities, and show its food in every the minutest fibre."

As I have begun to quote, I cannot deny myself the gratification of transcribing an admirable passage, in which the author feelingly denounces and exposes the attempts of the mischievous and heartless meddlers who are now tyrannising alike over poor and rich, who, hating all above, are applying the power extorted from the aristocracy to purposes to which the oligarchy would neither have desired *nor dared* to apply it,—to the coercion and frightful slavery of the poor.   But to my quotation:—

" If we hope to instruct others, we should familiarise our own minds to some *fixed* and *determinate* principles of action. The world is a vast labyrinth, in which almost every one is running a different way, and almost every one manifesting hatred to those who do not run the same way. A few, indeed, stand motionless, and, not seeking to lead themselves or others out of the maze, laugh at the failures of their brethren. Yet with little reason; for more grossly than the most bewildered wanderer does *he* err who never aims to go right. It is more honourable to the head, as well as to the heart, to be misled by our eagerness in the pursuit of truth, than to be safe from blundering by contempt of it. The happiness of mankind is the *end* of virtue, and truth is the knowledge of the *means,* which he will never seriously attempt to discover who has not habitually interested himself in the welfare of others. *The searcher after truth must love and be beloved,* for general benevolence is a necessary motive to constancy of pursuit; and this general benevolence is begotten and rendered permanent by social and domestic affections. *Let us beware of that reasoning which affects to inculcate philanthropy, while it denounces* EVERY HOME-BORN FEELING *by which it is produced and nurtured.* The paternal and filial duties discipline the heart and prepare it for the love of mankind. The intensity of private attachments encourages, not prevents, universal benevolence. The nearer we approach to the sun the more intense his heat; yet what corner of the system does he not cheer and vivify?"

Well do I recollect the very last conversation I had with my lamented friend. The projected Poor Law Bill was mentioned as an instance of the tyranny contemplated by the new parliament. He predicted that it would be carried. I remember that, in allusion to the system of coercive regulation which formed part of the bill by which all relief was denied at home, he made the affecting remark,—" *It is not bread alone, but the place where you eat it.*" He then, by a felicitous transition, turned to a beautiful tale of Tieck, in which there is an allusion to the question of pauperism, introduced by an affecting story of a beggar in Switzerland, who, being offended by a refusal where he had hitherto met with kindness, said, as he departed,—" Well, you will find I shall not come again, and then you may see if you can get another beggar." The whole is so admirably stated and reasoned, as well as felt, that, for the gratification as well as the profit of the ingenuous and affectionate natures to whom I address myself, I will extract the passage, premising only that the conversation is carried on at the table of an old counsellor, between old and young Eisenschlicht, Erich an old bachelor, Sophia, the daughter of the counsellor, and Edward, her suitor.

In reading this extract the reader will recognise, in the arguments and reasoning of old and young Eisenschlicht, a faint resemblance to the bolder daring of Lord Brougham and Chadwick, whilst in Edward and Sophia may be recognised a noble and high-purposed humanity which, however, has few counterparts in any of our public men.

" ' But why,' said Erich to his neighbour, ' are you disgusted with most of the works of the Flemish school here ?'

" ' Because they represent so many tatterdemalions and beggars,' answered the rich man. ' Nor are these Netherlanders the sole objects of my dislike: I hate particularly that Spaniard Murillo on that account, and even a great number of your Italians. It is melancholy enough that one cannot escape this vermin in the streets and market-places, nay, even in our very houses; but that an artist should require me besides to amuse myself with this noisome crew upon a motley canvas is expecting rather too much from my patience *.'

" ' Perhaps then,' said Edward, ' Quintin Matsys would suit you, who so frequently sets before us with

---

* This man was an economist of the worst kind, without knowing anything of political economy.

such truth and vigour money-changers at their counters, with coins and ledgers.'

" ' Not so either, young gentleman,' said the old man : ' that we can see easily and without exertion in reality. If I am to be entertained with a painting, I would have stately royal scenes, abundance of massy silk stuffs, crowns and purple mantles, pages and black-amoors; that, combined with a perspective of palaces and great squares, and down broad straight streets, elevates the soul ; it often puts me in spirits for a long time, and I am never tired of seeing it over and over again.'

" ' Undoubtedly,' said Erich, ' Paul Veronese, and several other Italians, have done many capital things in this department also.'

" ' What say you to a marriage of Cana in this manner ?' asked Edward.

" ' All eating,' replied the old man, ' grows tiresome in pictures, because it never stirs from its place ; and the roast peacocks and high-built pasties, as well as the cup-bearers half bent double, are in all such repre-sentations annoying things. But it is a different case when they are drawing a little Moses out of the water, and the king's daughter is standing by, in her most costly attire, surrounded by richly dressed ladies, who might themselves pass for princesses, men with halberds and armour, and even dwarfs and dogs : I cannot express how delighted I am when I meet with one of these stories, which in my youth I was forced to read in the uneasy confinement of a gloomy school-room, so gloriously dressed up. But you, my dear Mr. Walther, have too few things of this sort. Most of your pictures are for the feelings, and I never wish to be affected *, and least of all by works of art. Nor, indeed, am I ever so, but only provoked.'

" ' Still worse,' began young Eisenschlicht, ' is the case with our comedies. When we leave an agreeable company, and, after a brilliant entertainment, step into the lighted theatre, how can it be expected that we should interest ourselves in the variety of wretchedness and pitiful distress that is here served up for our amusement? Would it not be possible to adopt the same laudable regulation which is established by the police in most cities, to let me subscribe once for all for the relief of poverty, and then not be incommoded any farther by the tattered and hungry individuals?'

" ' It would be convenient, undoubtedly,' said Edward; ' but whether absolutely laudable, either as a regulation of police, or a maxim of art, I am not prepared to say. For my own part, I cannot resist a feeling of pity towards the individual unfortunates; and would not wish to do so, though to be sure one is often un-

---

* Just so.

seasonably disturbed, impudently importuned, and sometimes even grossly imposed upon.

" ' I am of your opinion,' cried Sophia : ' I cannot endure those dumb blind books, in which one is to write one's name, in order placidly to rely upon an invisible board of management, which is to relieve the distress as far as possible. In many places even it is desired that the charitable should engage to give nothing to individuals *. But how is it possible to resist the sight of woe? When I give to him who complains to me of his distress, I at all events see his momentary joy, and may hope to have comforted him.'

" ' This is the very thing,' said the old merchant, ' which in all countries maintains mendicity, that we cannot and will not rid ourselves of this petty feeling of soft-hearted vanity and mawkish philanthropy. This it is, at the same time, that renders the *better* † measures of states abortive and impracticable.'

" ' You are of a different way of thinking from those Swiss whom I have heard of,' said Edward. ' It was in a Catholic canton, where an old beggar had long been in the habit of receiving his alms on stated days,

* Surely H. B. must have read this.

† This is of the very essence of the new blasphemy. This general system will be found to require modification in a small parish of fifty souls. How can it be enforced throughout a whole nation without frightful suffering?—S. T. C.

and, as the rustic solitude did not allow much trade and
commerce, was accounted in almost every house one of
the family. It happened, however, that once, when he
called at a cottage where the inmates were extremely
busied in attending a woman in labour, in the confusion
and anxiety for the patient he met with a refusal.
When, after repeating his request, he really obtained
nothing, he turned angrily away, and cried as he departed, ' Well, 1 promise you, you shall find I do not
come again, and then you may see where you can catch
another beggar.' '

" All laughed, except Sophia, who would have it the
beggar's threat was perfectly rational, and concluded
with these words:—' Surely if it were put out of our
power to perform acts of benevolence, OUR LIFE ITSELF
WOULD BECOME POOR ENOUGH. If it were possible
that the impulse of pity could die in us, THERE WOULD
BE A MELANCHOLY PROSPECT FOR OUR JOY AND OUR
PLEASURE. *The man who is fortunate enough to be
able to bestow, receives more than the poor taker.
Alas! it is the only thing,*' she added with great emotion, ' *that can* AT ALL *excuse and mitigate the*
HARSHNESS OF PROPERTY, THE CRUELTY OF POS-
SESSION, that *a part* of what is *disproportionately
accumulated* is dropped upon the wretched creatures
who are pining below us, THAT IT MAY NOT BE

UTTERLY FORGOTTEN THAT WE ARE ALL BRE-
THREN*.'

" The father looked at her with a disapproving air,
and was on the point of saying something, when Edward, his beaming eyes fixed on the moist eyes of the
maid, interposed with vehemence: ' If the majority of
mankind were of the same way of thinking, we should
live in a different and a better world.   We are struck
with horror when we read of the distress that awaits the
innocent traveller in wildernesses and deserts of foreign
climes, or of the terrible fate which wastes a ship's crew
on the inhospitable sea, when, in their sorest need, no
vessel or no coast will appear on the immeasurable
expanse; we are struck with horror when monsters of
the deep tear to pieces the unfortunate mariner;—AND
YET, *do we not live in great cities, as upon the peak of
a promontory, where immediately at our feet all this
woe*, THE SAME HORRIBLE SPECTACLE DISPLAYS IT-

* I know nothing so ludicrous, and at the same time so
affecting, as this little incident and the after remarks of
Sophia. The very essence of femineity seems to speak in
the few and delicate, yet true and touching words. I am
not ashamed to say that when I first read them the tears
came into my eyes, and often, as I have read them since to
others, I cannot refrain from praying inwardly that the time
may be far distant when such sentiments shall be scouted by
our women.—S. T. C.

SELF, ONLY MORE SLOWLY, *and* THEREFORE *the more* CRUELLY*? But, from the midst of our concerts and banquets, and from the safe hold of our opulence, we look down into this abyss, where the shapes of misery† are tortured and wasted in a thousand fearful groups, as in Dante's imagery, AND DO NOT VENTURE EVEN TO RAISE THEIR EYES TO US, because *they* KNOW what a cold look they meet, when their cry rouses us at times out of the torpor of our cold apathy.'

" ' These,' said the elder Eisenschlicht, ' are youthful exaggerations. I still maintain, the really good citizen, the genuine patriot, ought not to suffer himself to be urged by a momentary emotion to support beggary. Let him bestow on those charitable institutions as much as he can conveniently spare; but let him not waste his slight means, which ought in this respect also to be subservient to the higher views of the state. For, in the opposite case, what is it he does? He promotes by his weakness—nay, I should be inclined to call it a voluptuous itching of the heart—imposture, laziness,

---

* Say selfishness, for the opulent have not a monopoly of cruelty.

† Say rather the punishments the selfish seek to inflict upon those by and through whom they have the opportunity of punishing. ALL men might be improvident, and ALL would be better if ALL were lavish, profuse, generous. It would not be possible for ALL to be selfish and grasping.— S. T. C.

and impudence, and withdraws his little contribution from real poverty, which, after all, he cannot always meet with or discern. Should we, however, be willing to acknowledge that overcharged picture of wretchedness to be correct, what good, even in this case, can a single individual effect? Is it in his power to improve the condition of the wretch who is driven to despair? What does it avail to give relief for a single day or hour? The unfortunate being will only feel his misery the more deeply, if he cannot change his state into a happy one; he will grow still more dissatisfied, still more wretched, and I injure instead of benefiting him.'

" ' Oh! do not say so,' exclaimed Edward, ' if you would not have me think harshly of you, for it sounds to me like blasphemy. *What the poor man gains in such a moment of sunshine! Oh! sir, he who is accustomed to be thrust out of the society of men;* he, for whom there is *no holiday, no market-place, no society,* AND SCARCELY A CHURCH; for whom ceremony, *courtesy,* and all the attentions which every man usually pays to his neighbour, are extinct; this wretched creature, for whom, *in public walks and vernal nature,* there shoots and blossoms *nothing but contempt,* often turns his dry eye to heaven and the stars above him, and sees there *even,* nothing but vacancy and doubts; *but in such an hour as that which unexpectedly bestows on him a more liberal boon,* and enables him to return to his gloomy hovel, to cheer his pining family with more than momentary comfort, faith in God, in his father, again rises in his heart, *he becomes once more a man, he feels again the neighbourhood of a brother, and can again love him and himself.* *Happy the rich man, who can promote this faith, who can bestow with the visible the invisible gift ; and woe to the prodigal, who, through his criminal thoughtlessness, deprives himself of those means of being a man among men ; for most severely will his feelings punish him, for having poured out in streams in the wilderness, like a heartless barbarian, the refreshing draught, of which a* SINGLE DROP *might have cheered his brother, who lay drooping under the load of his wearisome existence.'* He could not utter the last words without a tear ; he covered his face, and did not observe that the strangers and Erich had taken leave of their host. Sophia too wept ; but she roused herself and recovered her composure as her father returned."

LETTER IX.

31st July, 1820.

MY VERY DEAR FRIEND,

Before I opened your letter, or rather before I gave it to my best sister, and, under God, best comforter, to open, a heavy, a very heavy affliction came upon me with all the aggravations of surprise, sudden as a peal of thunder from a cloudless sky *

  *   *   *   *   *

    *   *   *   *

  *   *   *   *   *

    *   *   *   *

  *   *   *   *   *

Alas! both Mr. and Mrs. Gillman had spoken to him with all the earnestness of the fondest parents; his cousins had warned him, and I (long ago) had

---

* Here follows a detail of charges brought against one very near, and deservedly dear, to the writer, originating with, or adopted by the present Bishop of Llandaff. These charges were afterwards, I believe, withdrawn; at all events, compensation was tendered to the party implicated.

written to him, conjuring him to reflect with what a poisoned dagger it would arm my enemies: yea, and the phantoms that, half-*counterfeiting*, half-expounding the conscience, would persecute my sleep. My conscience indeed bears me witness, that from the time I quitted Cambridge, no human being was more indifferent to the pleasures of the table than myself, or less needed any stimulation to my spirits; and that by a most unhappy quackery, after having been almost bedrid for six months with swollen knees and other distressing symptoms of disordered digestive functions, and through that most pernicious form of ignorance, medical half-knowledge, I was *seduced* into the use of narcotics, not secretly, but (such was my ignorance) openly and exultingly, as one who had discovered, and was never weary of recommending, a grand panacea, and saw not the truth till my *body* had contracted a habit and a necessity; and that, even to the latest, my responsibility is for cowardice and defect of fortitude, not for the least craving after gratification or pleasurable sensation of any sort, but for yielding to pain, terror, and haunting bewilderment. But this I say to *man* only, who knows only what hás been yielded not what has been resisted ; before God I have but one voice — " Mercy! mercy! woe is me."—This was the sin of his nature, and this has been fostered by the culpable indulgence, at least non-interference, on my part; while, in a different quarter, contempt of the self-*interest* he saw seduced him unconsciously into *selfishness.*

Pray for me, my dear friend, that I may not pass such another night as the last. While I am awake and retain my reasoning powers, the pang is gnawing, but I am, except for a fitful moment or two, tranquil ; it is the howling wilderness of sleep that I dread.

I am most reluctant thus to transplant the thorns from my own pillow to yours, but sooner or. later you must know it, and how else could I explain to you the incapability I am under of answering your letter? For the present (my late visitation and sorrow out of the question) my anxiety is respecting your health. Mr. Gillman feels satisfied that there is nothing in your case symptomatic of aught more dangerous than irritable, and at present disordered, organs of digestion, requiring indeed great care, but by no means incompatible with comfortable health on the whole. Would to God! that your uncle lived near Highgate, or that we were settled near Clapham. Most anxious am I—(for I am sure I do not *overrate* Gillman's medical skill and sound medical good sense, and I have had every possible opportunity of satisfying myself on this head, *comparatively* as well as positively, from my intimate acquaintance with so many medical men in the course of my life)—I am most anxious that you should not apply to any medical practitioner at Clapham, till you have consulted some physician recommended by Gillman, and with whom our friend might have some confidential conversation.—The next earnest petition I make to you,— for should I lose *you* from this world, I fear that religious terrors would shake my strength of mind, and to how many are you, must you be, very dear, —is that you would stay in the country as long as is *morally* practicable. Let nothing but *coercive* motives have weight with you; a month's tranquil-

lity in pure air (O! that I could spend that month
with you, with no greater efforts of mental or bodily
exercise than would exhilarate both body and mind)
might save you many months' interrupted and half-
effective labour.

If any thoughts occur to you at Clapham on
which it would amuse or gratify you to have my
notions, write to me, and I shall be served by having something to think and write about not connected with myself.   But, at all events, write as
often as you can, and as much as (but not a syllable
more than) you ought.   Need I say how unspeak-
ably dear you are to your, you must not refuse me
to say in heart,

S. T. Coleridge.

This letter, interesting as it is to me from the
recollections and associations of those delightful
days, when its writer was to me a guide, philosopher, and, above and before all, a dear, very dear,
and valued friend, has an interest and a value
from the clear and simple account of his first using

laudanum. If any other testimony were or could be needed, I have received ample confirmation from subsequent communications. From this *bodily* slavery (*for it was bodily*) to a baneful drug, he was never *entirely* free, though the quantity was so greatly reduced as not materially to affect his health or spirits. For this alleviation he was indebted to the skill and attention of the medical friend of whom mention is made above, who, in a calling which, as at *present* pursued, tends more than perhaps any other *trade*, to degrade the moral being, has preserved a simplicity and singleness of purpose, united to a manly frankness, and combined with, or rather springing out of, a kindness and disinterestedness, which, as far as I have seen, has few equals. This excellent man seems to realise, in suburban practice, the example given in the following extract from the conversations of Coleridge :—

" The functions of a simple, earnest, and skilful country surgeon, living in a small town or village, and circulating in a radius of ten miles, are, and might *always* be made, superior in real, urgent, instant, and fitting relief, to the Lady Bountiful, and even to that of the Parson of the parish. I often think with pleasure of the active *practical* benevolence of Salter * His rides were often sixty, averaging more than thirty miles, every day, over bad roads and in dark nights; yet not once has he been known to refuse a summons, though quite sure that he would receive no remuneration, nay, not sure that it would not be necessary to supply wine or cordials, which, in the absence of the landlord of his village, must be at his own expense. This man was generally pitied by the affluent and the idle, on the score of his constant labours, and the drudgery which he almost seemed to court. Yet with little reason: for never knew I the man more to be envied, one more cheerful, more *invariably* kind, or more patient: always kind from real kindness and delicacy of feeling; never, even for a moment, angry. The present system of money-making, and, what is worse, slight of hand,

* Salter, if I recollect right, lived in Devonshire; but whether at Ottery or in its neighbourhood, I am ignorant.

and other tricks, for ostentation and stage effect leave little hope of future Salters."

As I have extracted a part, I will even give the remainder of the conversation of the day; one of those—alas! too few—which I have preserved at great length. Bitterly do I *now* regret, both for my own sake, and still more for yours, my dear children and youthful readers (for such chiefly do I wish), that a contempt for the character and pursuits of Boswell deterred me from making constant memorandums of conversations, which spread over a period of seventeen years, and, for a part of that time, almost daily, would now to me have been a treasure and a consolation unspeakable, in the dear and delightful recollections which they would have contained. These recollections, which are now so misty, so shadowy, and so unsubstantial, as to present little that is tangible, little that can be recalled bodily, would not be the less delightful to me as harmonising with the general character of my mind, if they did not also include regret the most poignant at the opportunities that I suffered to pass unimproved.

It may seem a contradiction, but I am never more grateful, never more thankful for the communion vouchsafed, never more revere the memory of the illustrious departed, than when I am compelled to come to conclusions directly opposed to those of the great teacher himself.

I have not observed the transitions from one subject to another; indeed, this was not possible without giving the whole conversation, with the remarks and observations of others—a course quite out of the question, seeing that each conversation would make a small volume; a volume, I may add, of great and most delightful interest throughout.

———————

" I believe that processes of thought might be carried on independent and apart from spoken or written language. I do not in the least doubt, that if language had been denied or withheld from man, or that he had not discovered and improved that mode of intercommunication, thought, as thought would have been a process more simple, more easy, and more perfect than at present, and would both have included and evolved other and better means for its own manifestations, than any that exist now."

" A clergyman has even more influence with the women than the handsome captain. The captain will captivate the fancy, whilst the young parson seizes upon the imagination, and subdues it to his service. The captain is *conscious* of his advantages, and sees the impression he has made long before his victim suspects the reality of any preference. The parson, unless he be the vain fop, for which, however, his education essentially unfits him, has often secured to himself the imagination, and, through the imagination, the best affections of those amongst whom he lives, before he is seriously attached himself."

" Hark yet again to that sweet strain! See how calm, how beauteous that prospect toward my garden! (thus he used sportively to call the demesne of Caen Wood, and its honest, though unreasoning owner, his head gardener). Would to God I could give out my being amidst flowers, and the sight of meadowy fields, and the chaunt of birds. Death without pain at such a time, in such a place as this, would be a reward for life. If I fear at all, I fear dying—I do not fear death."

" No, no; Lamb's scepticism has not come lightly, nor is he a sceptic. The harsh reproof to Godwin for his contemptuous allusion to Christ before a well-trained child, proves that he is not a sceptic. His mind, never prone to analysis, seems to have been disgusted with the hollow pretences, the false reasonings, and absurdities of the rogues and fools with which all establishments, and all creeds seeking to become established, abound. I look upon Lamb as one hovering between earth and heaven; neither hoping much nor fearing anything.

"It is curious that he should retain many usages which he learnt or adopted in the fervour of his early religious feelings, now that his faith is in a state of suspended animation. Believe me, who know him well, that Lamb, say what he will, has more of the *essentials* of Christianity than ninety-nine out of a hundred professing Christians. He has all that would still have been Christian had Christ never lived or been made manifest upon earth *."

"I deprecate a literal still more than an ideal religion. The miracles may be fairly illustrated by the familiar example of a lecture with experi-

* It will be interesting to compare Lamb's estimate of the belief of Coleridge—half serious, half sportive—with this defence of Lamb from the charge of scepticism. After a visit to Coleridge, during which the conversation had taken a religious turn, Leigh Hunt, after having walked a little distance, expressed his surprise that such a man as Coleridge should, when speaking of Christ, always call him our Saviour. Lamb, who had been exhilarated by one glass of that gooseberry or raisin cordial which he has so often anathematised, stammered out, "ne—ne—never mind what Coleridge says; he is full of fun."

ments at the institution. A man ignorant of the law whence these *conjurations* proceeded would be acted upon in a very different manner, when compared with the philosopher who, familiar with the law, or the principle whence they emanate, and with which they are congruous, sees in them only the natural results, hardly the confirmation of that which had previously been known. Compare this with the no-results obtained from meteorology, a science so misnamed, which so far from being in its infancy is not yet in its fetal state. The meteorological journals are as little to be relied upon, as would be the account of a ploughman, taken to an experimental lecture at the institution. Ignorant of the law and the principle he would give an account of the *results*, so different from the actual *facts*, that no one could conjecture a law from *his* evidence. So with the miracles. They are supererogatory. The law of God and the great principles of the Christian religion would have been the same had Christ never assumed humanity. It is for these things, and for such as these, for telling unwelcome truths, that I have been termed an atheist. It is for these opinions that William Smith assured the Archbishop of Canterbury that I was (what half the clergy are in *their lives*) an atheist. Little do these men know what atheism is. Not one man in a thousand has either strength of mind or goodness of heart to be an atheist. I repeat it. Not one man in ten thousand has goodness of heart or strength of mind to be an atheist.

" And, were I not a Christian, *and that only in the sense in which I am a Christian*, I should be an atheist with Spinosa; rejecting all in which I found insuperable difficulties, and resting my only hope in the *gradual, and certain because gradual, progression of the species*."

" This, it is true, is negative atheism; and this is, next to Christianity, the purest spirit of humanity!"

" Disliking the whole course and conduct of Carlile, I yet hold with him as against his judges and persecutors. I hold the assertion, that Christianity is part and parcel of the law of the land, to be an absurdity. It might as well be said because there is, or might be, a law to protect carpenters in the exercise of their trade, that architecture is part and parcel of the law. The government, or rather the party administering the functions of government, have never had the courage to place the question in its true light, and bring the action for a crime against society, not against *a creed*. When a man gives up the right of self-defence to a state, it is tacitly understood that the state undertakes to protect him equally against * *bodies* of men as against

---

* To explain this allusion it will be necessary to state that the prosecution against Carlile was carried on by a loyal and constitutional association; better known, at that time, as the Bridge-Street Gang. I have preserved an impromptu of Coleridge's, (which I wrote down at the time,) upon this body; the allusions in, and the application of, which, will be readily made by all interested.

> Jack Stripe
> Eats tripe,
> It is therefore credible
> That tripe is edible.
> And therefore perforce,
> It follows, of course,
> That the devil will gripe
> All who do not eat tripe.
>
> And as Nick is too slow
> To fetch em below,

individuals. Carlile *may be wrong; his persecutors undoubtedly are so.*"

" How I loathed the horrid speeches of the Attorney-General and of Mr. Justice Bayley, at the trial of that wretched man (Carlile). They said in so many words, ' The Unitarian who differs with you in nine points out of ten is sacred, but in the one point where he agrees with you, you condemn the deist.' Certainly the repeal of the act against unitarianism was entirely and unequivocally an acknowledgment that those points were not of moment. Carlile, if he had not been blinded by the steams arising from that hell, his own mind, might have taken advantage of this. Judge Abbot acted very well; he put the question on the ground of incivism, and not on the religious ground. No

> And Gifford, the attorney,
> Won't quicken the journey;
> The Bridge-Street Committee
> That colleague without pity,
> To imprison and hang
> Carlile and his gang,
> Is the pride of the city:
> And 'tis association
> That, alone, saves the nation
> From death and damnation."

doubt the early Christians, who in the second century threw down altars, attacked with uproar,
railing and abuse, the existing religion, are not to
be considered as martyrs, but as justly punished on
the ground of incivism; their conduct was contrary
to the injunction of their Great Master."

"The vulgar notion that a deist neither believes in
a future state nor in the existence of spirits is false,
according to the evidence of Christ himself; who
expressly says, when questioned on this point,
'Believe ye not this; neither would ye believe if
one were to rise from the dead.'   And again, 'No
man who believes not in this, is worthy to be
received.'"

"The paradox that the greater the truth the
greater the libel, has done much mischief. I had
once intended to have written a treatise on Phrases
and their Consequences, and this would have been
at the head. Certainly, if extended, it has some

truth; a man may state the truth in words, and yet tell a lie in spirit, and as such deserve punishment for calumny."

————

" All men in power are jealous of the pre-eminence of men of letters; they feel, as towards them, conscious of inferior power, and a sort of misgiving that they are, *indirectly, and against their own will, mere instruments and agents of higher intellects.*

Men in power, for instance Lord Castlereagh, are conscious of inferiority, and are yet ashamed to own, even to themselves, the fact, which is only the more evident by their neglect of men of letters. So entirely was Mr. Pitt aware of this that he would never allow of any intercourse with literary men of eminence; fearing, doubtless, that the charm which spell-bound his political adherents would, at least for *the time*, fail of its effect."

————

" There is a great, a general want of intellect at this time, so much so that when any convulsion occurs, *it will tell fatally*. The fabric of our society resembles a house of cards built by children, which so long as the squares support a roof, and that roof an angle, and the inter-dependence is sufficient all seems well; but the moment the fabric is shaken, and when the component parts can no longer form an angle, it will assuredly fall to the ground. See First Lay Sermon. The Second Lay Sermon, and the Letters to Judge Fletcher are, in truth, wonderful prophecies."

" If I should finish ' Christabel,' I shall certainly extend it and give new characters, and a greater number of incidents. This the ' reading public' require, and this is the reason that Sir Walter Scott's poems, though so loosely written, are pleasing, and interest us by their picturesqueness.

" If a genial recurrence of the ray divine should occur for a few weeks, I shall certainly attempt it. I had the whole of the two cantos in my mind before I began it; certainly the first canto is more perfect, has more of the true wild weird spirit than the last. I laughed heartily at the continuation in Blackwood, which I have been told is by Maginn : it is in appearance, and in appearance *only*, a good imitation; I do not doubt but that it gave more pleasure, and to a greater number, than a continuation by myself in the *spirit* of the two first cantos.

" The ' Ancient Mariner' cannot be imitated, nor the poem, ' Love.' *They may be excelled; they are not imitable.*"

" Peter's Letters to his Kinsfolk * seem to have

* I have extracted from the above work the following tribute to the genius of Coleridge by Professor Wilson, *clarum et venerabile nomen.*

" If there be any man of grand and original genius alive at this moment, in Europe, it is Coleridge; nothing can surpass the melodious richness of words which he heaps around his images—images which are not glaring in themselves, but which are always affecting to the very verge of tears, because they have all been formed and nourished in the recesses of one of the most deeply musing spirits that ever breathed forth its inspirations in the majestic language of England. Who that ever read Genevieve can doubt this? That poem is known to all readers of poetry, although comparatively few of

originated in a sort of familiar conversation between
two clever men, who have said, 'Let us write a
book that will sell; you write this, and I will
write that,' and in a sort of laughing humour set to
work.   This was the way that Southey and myself
wrote many things together."

"I am glad you are now to see the Wallenstein
for the first time, as you will then see a specimen
of my happiest attempt, during the prime manhood
of my intellect, before I had been buffeted by
adversity or crossed by fatality.   The 'Remorse'
is certainly a great favourite of mine, the more so

them are aware that it is the work of Coleridge.   His love-
poetry is, throughout, the finest that has been produced in
England since the days of Shakspeare and the old dramatists.
The old dramatists, and Coleridge, regard women with far
higher reverence—far deeper insight into the true grandeur
of their gentleness.   I do not think there is any poet in the
world who ever touched so truly the mystery of the passion
as he has done in *Genevieve*, and in that other exquisite poem
where he speaks of

> Her voice—
> Her voice, that, even in its mirthful mood,
> Hath made me wish to steal away and weep."

as certain pet abstract notions of mine are therein expounded."

———————

" Mr. Green is indeed a worthy man, at least so all my friends say. Bred up from the age of twelve in a hospital, he has yet not failed to shun their horrid materialism. He has come to a very different conclusion to that at which most other operators, most psychologists have arrived. He has been able to believe in a spiritual first cause and in a presiding free will. This you will see in his preface*.

" I deplore in my inmost heart the present mental degradation of E., who, not contented with denying the primal truths of religion and the divine nature of man, holds opinions which were *ever* considered as base, hateful, and to be abhorred; opinions which degrade man below the beast. Quoted that passage of Cicero, wherein he says,—" Concerning

* It is to be hoped that Mr. Green will favour the world with the process by which he has arrived at these conclusions.

these things there are (or may be) different opinions;
but those who disbelieve the existence of goodness,
not only from the want of it themselves but after
much consideration, are to be held as out of the
pale of society.'"

***

"Tobin came one morning with a face of much
interest to inform me that Davy had made a wonderful discovery.   'I doubt it not; I think he
will make many discoveries.'   'Yes, yes; but I
mean in philosophy.   He tells me he has discovered that it is *possible* there may be a God!'"

***

"I once asked Tom Clarkson whether he ever
thought of his probable fate in the next world, to
which he replied, 'How can I? I think only of
the slaves in Barbadoes!' Does Mr. Wilberforce
care a farthing for the slaves in the West Indies, or
if they were all at the devil, so that *his soul were
saved?*

"As there is a worldliness or the *too-much* of this

life, so there is *another-worldliness*, or rather *other worldliness*, equally hateful and selfish with *this worldliness*."

———————

" Lord Erskine, speaking of animals, hesitating to call them brutes, hit upon that happy phrase— ' the mute creation.' "

———————

" Lord Kenyon, on the trial of a bookseller, for publishing ' Paine's Age of Reason,' in his charge to the jury, enumerated many celebrated men who had been sincere Christians; and, after having enforced the example of Locke and Newton,—both of whom were Unitarians, and therefore not Christians,—proceeded:—' Nor, gentlemen, is this belief confined to men of comparative seclusion, since men, the greatest and most distinguished both as philosophers and as monarchs, have enforced this belief, and shown its influence by their conduct. Above all, gentlemen, need I name to you the Emperor Julian, who was so celebrated for the practice of every Christian virtue that he was called Julian the Apostle*.'"

"It is indisputable that nervous excitation is con- tagious. The greater part of ghost stories may be traced to this source."

"Forms exist before the substance out of which they are shaped."

"One thought includes all thought in the sense that a grain of sand includes the universe.

"I hold with St. Paul that charity is the greatest of the virtues. Original sin is best explained by depravation of the will. Calvinism, or the belief

---

* This most extraordinary blunder must have arisen from the judge's reading having been more select than various. It is probable that all the knowledge he had of Julian was picked out of 'Fielding's Journey to the Next World,' which, however, he seems not to have understood.

in election, is not simply blasphemy, but super-fetation of blasphemy."

———

" For one person who has remarked or praised a beautiful passage in Walter Scott's works, a hundred have said,—' How many volumes he has written ! ' So of Mathews : it is not ' How admirable such and such parts are ! ' but ' It is wonderful that one man should do *all this !* ' "

———

LETTER X.

August 8th, 1820.

MY VERY DEAR FRIEND,

Neither indolence nor procrastination have had any place among the causes of my silence, least of all either yourself, or the subject of your letter, or the purpose of answering it, having been absent from my thoughts. You may with almost literal truth attribute it to want of time, from the

number, quantity, and quality of my engagements,
the necessity of several journeys *to* and (still worse)
in town being the largest waster of time and
spirits. At length I have settled J. for the next six
or eight weeks with Mr. Montague, where he is
engaged on an Essay on the Principles of Taste
in relation to Metre and Rhythm, containing, first,
a new scheme of prosody, as applied to the choral
and lyrical stanzas of the Greek drama; secondly,
the possibility of improving and enriching our English versification by digging in the original mines,
viz.—the tunes of nature and impassioned conversation, both of which may be illustrated from
Mr. Frere's* Aristophanic Poems. I have been

---

* As these poems, the precursors of "Beppo" and "Don
Juan," are not now in general circulation, I subjoin two
short extracts, one a sketch of a gallant knight; the second
showing the advantage of being well victualled.

On every point, in earnest and in jest,
His judgment, and his prudence, and his wit
Were deemed the very touchstone and the text
Of what was proper, graceful, just, and fit.
A word from him set everything at rest,
His short decisions never failed to hit;
His silence, his reserve, his inattention,
Were felt as the severest reprehension.

working hard to bring together for him the notes, &c., that I had prepared on this subject. E. has been ill, and even now is far from well. There are

His memory was the magazine and hoard
Where claims and grievances, from year to year,
And confidences and complaints were stored,
From dame and knight, from damsel, boor, and peer ;
Loved by his friends, and trusted by his lord,
A generous courtier, secret and sincere,
Adviser-general to the whole community,
He served his friend, but watched his opportunity.

———————

For, in the garrison where he presided,
Neither distress, nor famine, nor disease
Were felt, nor accident nor harm betided
The happy monk ; but plenteous, and with ease,
All needful monkish viands were provided ;
Bacon and pickled herring, pork and peas ;
And, when the table-beer began to fail,
They found resources in the bottled ale.

Dinner and supper kept their usual hours,
Breakfast and luncheon never were delayed,
While to the sentries on the walls and towers,
Between two hot plates, messes were conveyed.
At the departure of the invading power,
It was a boast the noble abbot made,
None of his monks were weaker, paler, thinner,
Or, during all the siege, had lost a dinner.

some persons—I have known several—who, when they find themselves uncomfortable, take up the pen and transfer as much discomfort as they can to their absent friends. But I know only one of this sort, who, as soon as they take up the pen, instantly become *dolorous*, however smug, snug, and cheerful the minute before and the minute after.

Now just such is Mrs. D., God bless her! and she has been writing letter after letter to E. about J., and every discomfortable recollection and anticipation that she could conjure up, that she has completely overset him. *This must not be.* Mr. Gillman, too, has been *out* of *sorts*, but at this present we are all better. I at least am as well as I ever am, and my regular employment, in which Mr. Green is weekly my amanuensis, the work on the books of the Old and New Testaments, introduced by the assumptions and postulates required as the pre-conditions of a fair examination of Christianity as a scheme of doctrines, precepts, and histories, drawn or at least deducible from these books. And now, in the narrative line, I have only to add that

Mrs. Gillman desires to be affectionately remembered to you, and bids me entreat you to stay *away as long* as you possibly can, provided it be from *London* as well as from Highgate.

Would to heaven I were with you! In a few days you should see that the spirit of the mountaineer is not yet utterly extinct in me. Wordsworth has remarked (in the Brothers, I believe),

" The thought of death sits light upon the man
   That has been bred, and dies among the mountains."

But I fear that this, like some other few of Wordsworth's *many* striking passages, means less than it seems, or rather promises, to mean. Poets (especially if philosophers too) are apt to represent the effect made upon themselves as general; the geese of Phœbus are all swans; and Wordsworth's shepherds and estates men are Wordsworth's, even (as in old Michael) in the unpoetic traits of character. Whether mountains have any particular effect on the native inhabitants by virtue of being mountains exclusively, and what that effect is, would be a difficult problem. If independent tribes, moun-

taineers are robbers of the lowlanders; brave,
active, and with all the usual warlike good and bad
qualities that result from habits of adventurous
robbery. Add clanship and the superstitions that are
the surviving *precipitate* of an established religion,
both which are common to the uncivilised Celtic
tribes, in plain no less than in mountain, and you
have the Scottish Highlanders. But where the
inhabitants exist as states, or civilised parts of civilised states, they appear to be in mind and character just what their condition and employments
would render them in level plain, the same as amid
Alpine heights. At least the influence acts indirectly only, as far as the mountains are the *causa
causæ* or occasion of a *pastoral* life instead of an
agricultural; thus combining a lax and common
property, possessed by a whole district, with small
hereditary estates sacred to each, while the proper-
ties in sheep seem to partake of both characters.
And truly, to this circumstance, aided by the favour-
able action of a necessarily scanty population (for
man is an oak that wants room, not a *plantation
tree*), we must attribute whatever superiority the

mountaineers of Cumberland and Westmoreland and of the Swiss and Tyrolese Alps possess, as the shocking contrast of the Welsh mountaineers too clearly evinces. But this subject I have discussed, and (if I do not flatter myself) satisfactorily, in the Literary Life, and I will not conceal from *you* that this inferred dependency of the human soul on accidents of birth-place and abode, together with the vague, misty, rather than mystic, confusion of God with the world, and the accompanying nature-worship, of which the asserted dependence forms a part, is the trait in Wordsworth's poetic works that I most dislike as unhealthful, and denounce as contagious; while the odd introduction of the popular, almost the vulgar, religion in his later publications (the popping in, as Hartley says, of the old man with a beard), suggests the painful suspicion of worldly prudence—at best a justification of masking truth (which, in fact, is a falsehood substituted for a truth withheld) on plea of expediency—carried into religion. At least it conjures up to my fancy a sort of *Janus* head of Spinosa and Dr. Watts, or " I and my brother the dean."

Permit me, then, in the place of the two lines,

" The thought of death sits easy on the man
Who hath been bred, and dies among the mountains,"

to say,

" The thought of death sits easy on the man,
Whose earnest *will* hath lived among the deathless."

And I can perhaps build upon this foundation an answer to the question, which would deeply interest me, by whomever put, and pained me only because it was put by *you ; i. e.* because I feared it might be the inspiration of ill health, and am jealous of any *consenting* of that inward will which, with some mysterious germination, moves in the Bethesda pool of our animal life, to withdraw its resistance. For the soul, among its other regalia, has an energetic veto against all undermining of the constitution, and among these, as not the least insidious, I consider the thoughts and hauntings that tamper with the love of life.

Do not so ! you *would not*, if I could transfer into you, in all its depth and liveliness, the sense what a hope, promise, impulse, you are to me in my present efforts to realise my past labours; and by building up the temple,—the shaped stones, beams, pillars, yea, the graven ornaments and the connecting clamps of which have been piled up by me, only in too great abundance,—to enable you and my two (may I not say other) sons to affirm, —*Vivit, quia non frustra vixit.*

In reading an extract in the German Encyclopœdia from Dobrizhoffer's most interesting account of the Abiponenses, a savage tribe in Paraguay, houseless, yet in person and in morals the noblest of savage tribes; who, when first known by Europeans, amounted to 100,000 warriors, yet have a tradition that they were but the relic of a far more numerous community, and who by wars with other savage tribes, and by intestine feuds among themselves, are now dwindled to a thousand (men, women, and children do not exceed five thousand), it struck me with distinct remembrance—first, that this is the history of *all* savage tribes; and, second, that all tribes *are* savage that have not a positive religion defecated from witchcraft, and an established priesthood contra-distinguished from indivi-

dual conjurers. Nay, the islands of the Pacific
(the Polynesia, which sooner or later the swift and
silent masonry of the coral worms will compact
into a rival continent, into a *fifth quarter* of the
world), blest with all the plenties of nature, and
enjoying an immunity from all the ordinary dangers
of savage life, were many of them utterly dispeopled
since their first discovery, and wholly by their own
feuds and vices ; nay, that their bread fruit tree and
their delicious and healthful climate had only made
the process of mutual destruction and self-destruction
more hateful, more basely sensual. This, therefore,
I assume as an undoubted fact of history ; and
from this, as a portion of the history of *men*, I draw
a new (to my knowledge, at least, a new) series of
proofs of several, I *might* say of *all*, the positions
of pre-eminent importance and interest more than
vital ; a series which, taken in harmonious counter-
part to a prior series drawn from *interior* history
(the history of *man*), the documents of which are to
be found only in the archives of each individual's
own consciousness, will form a complete *whole*—a
system of evidence, consisting of two correspondent

worlds, as it were, correlative and mutually poten-
tiating, yet each integral and self-subsistent—having
the same correlation, as the geometry and the observations, or the metaphysics and the physics, of
astronomy. If I can thus demonstrate the truth of
the doctrine of existence after the present life, it is
not improbable that some rays of light may fall on
the question, what *state* of existence it may be rea-
sonably supposed to be ? At all events, we shall,
I trust, be enabled to determine negatively, what it
can *not* be for *any* ; and *for whom* this or that,
which does not appear universally precluded, is yet
for them precluded. In plainer words, what can
not be, universally speaking ; second, what may be ;
third, what the differences may be for different
individuals, within the limits prescribed in No. 2 ;
fourth, what scheme of embodied representation of
the future state (our *reason* not forbidding the same)
is recommended by the truest analogies ; and, fifth,
what scheme it is best to combine with our belief of
a hereafter, as most conducive to the growth and
cultivation of our collective faculties in this life, or
of each in the order of its comparative worth, value,

and permanence. This I must defer to another letter, for I cannot let another post pass by, without your knowing that we are all thinking of and loving you.

S. T. COLERIDGE.

To the preceding letter, pregnant as it is with materials for thinking, your attention will be attracted, both by the great variety of subjects brought forward and illustrated, and by the expressions of earnest and affectionate attachment which it contains.

Certainly no man that I ever knew united in so great a degree, *so entirely*, "fondeur" with the most extreme simplicity, and the most artless and confiding affection. The whole craving of his moral being was for love. Who is not affected, what man does not grieve, when he hears him exclaim—

> " *To be* BELOVED *is* ALL *I need,*
>   *And whom I* LOVE, *I* LOVE *indeed.*"

> " Why was I made for love, and love denied to me?"

Alas! my dear children, how can I hope to convey to you (except your own minds are consenting) all that this glorious being was to me in the days when his *vast* intellect was in its most gorgeous manhood, and I was yet in the first singleness, and, I will add, purity, of mind.

" Few, and far between," are the moments when I can recal that other self, which, in days past, sat at the feet of the greatest of moderns—that seemed to unite energy, variety, a mind eminently suggestive, with an affection and a reverence, without any assignable limits, for whatever was beautiful and loveable in man or in external nature,

" Who was retired as noon-tide dew,
    Or fountain in a noon-day grove;
And you must love him, ere to you
    He will seem worthy of your love.

" The outward shows of sky and earth,
    Of hill and valley he has viewed ;
And impulses of deeper birth
    Have come to him in solitude.

" In common things that round us lie,
    Some random truths he can impart,
The harvest of a quiet eye,
    That broods and sleeps on his own heart.

" But he is shy, both man and boy
    Hath been an idler in the land ;
Contented, if he might enjoy
    The things that others understand."

The next letter, which contained the farther development of the very interesting matters opened in the preceding letter, I have mislaid, or, I much fear, lost.

LETTER XI.

Highgate, Oct. 11th, 1820.

MY DEAR FRIEND,

You will think it childish in me, and more savouring of a jealous boarding-school miss than a friend and a philosopher, when I confess that the " with great respect, your obliged and grateful . . ," gave me pain. But I did not return from Mr. Cooper's, at whose house we all dined, till near midnight, and did not open the packet till this morning after getting out of bed; and this you know is the hour in which the cat-organ of an irritable viscerage is substituted for the brain as the mind's instrument.

The Cobbett is assuredly a strong and battering production throughout, and in the best bad style of this political rhinoceros, with his coat armour of dry and wet mud, and his one horn of brutal strength on the nose of scorn and hate; not to forget the flaying rasp of his tongue! There is one article of his invective, however, from which I cannot withhold my vote of consent: that I mean which respects Mr. Brougham's hollow complimentary phrases to the ministry and the House of Lords. On expressing my regret that his poor hoaxed and hunted client had been lured or terrified into the nets of the revolutionists, and had taken the topmost perch, as the flaring, screaming *maccaw* in the clamorous aviary of faction, Sheriff Williams, who dined with us, premising that his *wishes* accorded with mine, declared himself, however, fully and deeply convinced, that, without this alliance, the Queen must have been overwhelmed, not wholly or even chiefly from the strength of the party itself, but because, without the activity, enthusiasm, and combination, peculiar to the reformists, her case, in all its detail and with all its appendages, would never have had that notoriety so beyond example universal; which (to translate Sheriff Williams into Poet Coleridge), with kettle-drum reveillée, had echoed through the mine and the coal-pit, which had lifted the latch of every cottage, and thundered with no run-away knock at Carlton Palace. I could only reply, that I had never yet seen, heard, or read of any advantage in the long run, occurring to a good cause from an unholy alliance with evil passions and incongruous or alien purposes. It was ever heavy on my heart, that the people, alike high and low, do perish for lack of knowledge; that both sheep and shepherd, the Flocks and the Pastors, go astray among swamps and in desolate places, for want of the *Truth*, the *whole* Truth, and nothing but the Truth; and that the sacred motto, which I had adopted for my first political publication (The Watchman), would be the aspiration of my death-bed—THAT ALL MAY KNOW THE TRUTH; AND THAT THE TRUTH MAY MAKE US FREE.

I observed farther, that in bodies of men, not accidentally collected nor promiscuously, but such as our House of Lords, the usual effect of terror was, first, self-justification as to the worst of their past violent and unconstitutional measures; and, next, a desperate belief that their safety would be still more endangered by giving way than by plunging onward;—that, if they must fall, they would fall in that way in which they might take vengeance on the occasion of the mischief. If the proposition be either . . . or . . . , and the latter blank is to be filled up by *a Civil War*, what shall we put for the former, to make our duty to submit to it deniable or even doubtful? A Legislature permitted by us to stand in the eye of the whole civilised World as the representative of our country, corruptly and ruthlessly pandering to an Individual's Lust and Hate! Open Hostility to Innocence, and the subversion of justice, a shameless trampling under foot of the Laws of God and the Principles of the Constitution, in the name and against the known will of the Nation! Well! if anything, it must be this! It is a decision, compared with which the sentence of the elder Brutus were a grief for which an onion might supply the tears. A dreadful decision! But be it so!—How much more then are we bound to be careful, that no conduct of our own, no assent or countenance given by us to the violence of others, no want of courage and alertness in denouncing the same, should have the least tendency to bring about an act or event, dire enough to justify a civil war for its preventive? I produced, as you may suppose, but small effect; and yet your very note enforces the truth of my reply—for these very answers of the Queen's conjointly with her plebicolar (or plebicolous) Clap-Trapperies in the live puppet-shew of wicked Punch and his wife, that has come back again, and the devil on all sides, make it impossible for me to ask you, as I otherwise should have done,—What proof, proveably independent of the calumny plot, have we of any want of delicacy in the Queen? What act or form of demeanour can be adduced on competent testi-mony, from which we are forced or entitled to infer innate Coarseness, if not Grossness? The dire disclosure of the extent and extremes to which Calumny may be carried—and perhaps the recent persecution of poor dear . . . . . mixes its workings—makes me credulous in incredulity; so that I am almost prepared to reverse the proverb, and think that "what every one says must be a lie!" They put a body up to the nostrils in the dung-hill of reeking slander, and then exclaim: There is no smoke without some fire!

It is my purpose, God willing! to leave this place on Friday, so as to take an afternoon coach, if any such there be, or the Oxford mail, as the dernier resource—and so to be in Oxford by Saturday morning, while my letter, which is unfortunately a very long one (and I could not make it otherwise), will reach Dr. Copplestone, if arrived, on Friday morning; thus giving him a day's preparation for the personal interview. How long my absence from Highgate may be, I cannot of course predetermine; certainly not an hour beyond what . . . . . 's interest requires.

God bless you, my dear friend, and your truly

affectionate, and—if it did not look like a *retort,*
how truly might I not add—

     Your obliged and grateful friend,

          S. T. COLERIDGE.

P. S. Sheriff Williams is apparently a very
worthy, and assuredly a very entertaining man.
He gave us accounts, on his own evidence, of
wonderful things respecting Miss M'Evoy and a
Mr. De Vains of Liverpool; so wonderful as to
threaten the stoppage even of my Bank of Faith.

I have just heard from Derwent, who is well;
but I have not had time to decipher his villainous
scrawl.

I wish it was possible for me to give even a faint
notion of the splendid eloquence of my friend on
this topic. The interest he took in this great question on all occasions, induced me to entreat *repeatedly*
that he would embody his views and opinions in a
pamphlet, to be called " Thoughts on the Present

Persecution;" but better, certainly more prudent, counsels prevailed.

On the conduct of Mr. Brougham in this case, he was accustomed to animadvert with great severity. His great and constant indiscretions, and, above all, an insincerity, which then seemed to have an object, but which greater experience has shown to arise from want of Ballast, in short (why should I not say it?) from mental unsoundness, were at that time matters of deep regret to all right-minded men.

It is painful thus to speak of a man variously gifted, and possessed unquestionably of great talents; but it is needful to bear in mind, that though men of restless natures and irritable temperaments have frequently been the instruments of functional improvements, they are totally unsuited to times which require organic changes. If this be the case with regard to men who are restless from enthusiasm, or whose fermentation arises from the crude state of their minds, and respecting whom there is yet hope when experience shall have mellowed their convictions; what shall we say of those, to whom time brings no improvement—age, no mental repose? It is the duty of all men, who have calmly observed, meditated, and reflected, who are sufficiently near to be interested, and remote enough for quiet contemplation, to put their testimony on record; which, though it may not avail in the present times, will yet serve as a time-mark for the future.

Yet I can never believe but that a man so variously gifted, must, at some time or other, have had aspirations of a higher and purer nature than should seem possible, judging of the turmoil and turbulence of his latter career. Hear what is thought of this man by an accomplished foreigner. In a letter of Jacquemont's, written from the Himalaya, are the following reflections, which are but too just. " I have just read the sixteen immense columns of Lord Brougham's speech on 7th Oct. 1831. What talents! but what a perverted use of talent. What a disagreeable kind of talent is that, which disgusts the hearer instead of conciliating him. If I were a public man, I would study Brougham, *not* to resemble him. What is the *use* of that cutting irony, that bitter sarcasm, that supercilious pride? What is the *use* of those Greek and Latin verses?"

I must also protest against the terms employed, in speaking of the very extraordinary man lately lost to that country he so dearly loved, and for the welfare of which country, and those who lived upon it and by it, his last words were uttered.

A man more kind-hearted, *more kindly*, I never knew. That he was intolerant, turbulent, and domineering, I admit freely, but towards whom? To those only who were self-seekers, proud, narrow in their views, and, above all, to those who sought to oppress and degrade that great class from which he sprung, and with which he gloried to identify himself.

To the concluding portion of this letter it will be needless to point attention. Like every thing my friend wrote, it is for all time, and would be equally applicable in its spirit under any conceivable form of society.

The American coachman, who, to the great

surprise of Mr. Stewart, told him more of the
practice and mode of teaching at the High School
of Edinburgh than he knew himself, although
educated* at that school, justly observed that
the two great principles which have divided and
still divide mankind, are eternal, and not dependent
upon the names with which they are associated.
Substituting only the words " true Reformer" for
" Whig " (for *here* the Whigs are not *true* Re-
formers), I know not a more just observation.
" In truth, the parties of Whig and Tory are those
of Nature. They exist in all countries, whether
called by those names or by those of aristocrats
and democrats, *côté droite* and *côté gauche*, ultras

---

* When Lord Stanley was in America, it was necessary to
speak of the General Post Office: he did not know where it
was ; whilst a judge who was at the table pointed out its
exact situation in Lombard-street, and evinced so much local
knowledge, that Lord Stanley said,—" You must have been
a long time in London, ———?" " I was never there in my
life," was the reply.

See here the difference. The American had informed
himself of that which he was not expected to know, which it
was excusable in him not to know ; whilst the aristocrat was
ignorant of that which it was incumbent upon him to have
known.

and radicals, serviles and liberals. The sickly, weakly, timid man fears the people, and is a Tory by nature; the healthy, strong, and bold man cherishes them, and is a Whig by nature." It is well that the people of England are not educated to any knowledge of their political rights, or the scandalous frauds of the past year would have met their fitting punishments. How long will the manly and mature intellect of this great mother, *this great hive*, of nations submit to the guidance of *litterateurs* and lordlings, who, by virtue of pretension and prescription alone, are held to be fit to govern *nations*, though there are *few men* in the present cabinet to whom a merchant would intrust a ship, a farmer employ as a bailiff, or a draper engage as an assistant, even were their services offered gratuitously.

LETTER XII.

Saturday, Oct. 20th, 1820.

MY DEAR FRIEND,

Doubtless nothing can be more delightful to me, independent of Mrs. Gillman's kind but unnecessary anxieties, than to go to Oxford with you. Nay, though it will be but a flight to and fro, with a sojourn but of two days, if so much, yet I should even ask it of you if I were quite sure, absolutely sure, that it would not inconvenience you.

But in the fear of this, I could not ask or receive your companionship without some selfishness which would completely baffle itself.

I have not yet received an answer from Oxford respecting Dr. Coplestone's return to Oriel.

God bless you, my ever dear friend,

S. T. COLERIDGE.

Of this journey to Oxford I have a very painful recollection; perhaps the most painful recollection (one excepted) connected with the memory of Coleridge. Still I think that the journey was beneficial to his health, and that he was better for some weeks after his return.

" A single thought is that which it is from other thoughts, as a wave of the sea takes its form and shape from the waves which precede and follow it."

" In the system of gravity, Newton only developed the idea of Kepler. He advanced a step, and there he fixed his followers. Kepler would have pro-gressed, or have been stationary in act at least."

LETTER XIII.

Oct. 25th, 1820.

MY DEAREST FRIEND,

It will please you, though I scarcely know whether the pleasure is worth the carriage, to know that my own feelings and convictions were, from the very commencement of this unhappy affair, viz.—the terms proposed to the Queen by Lord Hutchinson, in coincidence with your present suggestion, and that I actually began an essay, and proposed a sort of *diary*, *i. e.* remarks moral and political, according as the events of the day suggested them. But Mr. Gillman dissuaded me. Again, about five weeks ago I had written a letter to Conder, the editor of the Eclectic Review and *ci-devant* bookseller, offering, and offering to *execute*, a scheme of publication, " the Queen's case stated *morally*; 2, judicially; 3, politically." But *again* Mr. G. earnestly persuaded me to suppress it.   His reasons were, first, that my mind was not sufficiently tranquil, in consequence of I.'s affair, to enable me to rely upon going through with the publication; secondly, that it would probably involve me with certain of my connexions in high life, and be injurious to Hartley and Derwent, especially the latter; with, thirdly, the small chance of doing any good, people are so guided by their first notions.   To tell you the truth, Mr. G.'s *own dislike* to it was of more weight than all his three reasons.

However, we will talk of the publication, if *it be not too late*, and at all events I will compose the statement.

I pray you make no apologies for doing that which cannot but add to the esteem and affection with which I am most truly your *friend,* fraternally and paternally,

S. T. COLERIDGE.

We shall soon see you?

Shortly after this I find the following heads of conversation :—

" I recollect meeting Mr. Brougham well. I met him at Mr. Sharp's with Mr. Horner. They were then aspirants for political adventures. Mr. Horner bore in his conversation and demeanour evidence of that straight-forward and generous frankness which characterised him through life. You saw, or rather you felt, that you could rely upon *his* integrity. His mind was better fitted to reconcile discrepancies than to discover analogies. He had fine, nay, even high, talent rather than genius. Mr. Brougham, on the contrary, had an apparent restlessness, a consciousness, not of superior powers, but of superior activity, a man whose heart was placed in what should have been his head: you were never sure of him—you always doubted his sincerity. He was at that time a hanger-on upon Lord Holland, Mr. Horner being under the auspices of Lord Lansdowne.

" From that time I lost sight of Mr. Brougham for some time. When we next met, the subject of the parliamentary debates was alluded to, previously to which Mr. Brougham had expressed opinions which were in unison with my own upon a matter at that time of great public interest.

" I said ' I could never rely upon what was given for the future in the newspapers, as they had made him say directly the contrary; I was glad to be undeceived.'

" 'Oh,' said Brougham, in a tone of voice half confidential and half jocular, ' Oh, it was very true I said so in Parliament, where there is a party, but *we* know better.'

" *I said nothing ; but I did not forget it.*"

" The question of the atonement and of the sacrament being introduced, he insisted on the divine origin of the sacrament, and that it was to be understood in a mystical sense, not, however, as a real presence. It has very clearly relation to the sixth chapter of John; nay, Clement expressly affirms it to be a solemn mysterious ceremony, in which he is sustained by Justin Martyr. With respect to free will, in the ordinary acceptation, he affirmed it to be incompatible with omnipotence, with the attributes of that God who is omniscient and omnipresent, who is in all things, and in whom all things are, to whom time past and time to come ever *is*. Man is not to be saved without *his* saving grace."

" Speaking of the term 'Son of Man,' taken literally by the Socinians, he said,—' The Son of Man! What is it but mockery if he were really a man, the man Jesus Christ. He was incarnate in Trinity or tri-unity; first, he was incarnate as the Logos, or Word, next, he was incarnate with the Holy Spirit unto all things, that he might remain in the spirit; and, lastly, he was incarnate in his humanity.' "

" Compared to the Jewish law, given as it was in thunders and in terrible convulsions of the elements, the miracles of the Christian dispensation were devoid of interest.

" There can be no doubt that a religion like that

of the Jews, a religion of punishments and threatenings only, was incomplete; it must, *therefore*, be false, or it required to be perfected."

———

" Speaking of Baxter, he affirmed that he was a century before his time, that he was a logician, and first applied the tri-fold or tri-une demonstration. Heretofore, the two-fold method only was known as the arguing from a positive to a negative, the reality *ergo* the visionary. He also first introduced the method of argument, that the thing or reason given contains a positive and its opposite; *ex. gr.*, reality contains the actual and the potential, as, I sit, the actual, but I have the power, the potentiality, of walking. Baxter tried to reconcile the almost irreconcilable tenets of Calvinism and Arminianism. He more than any other man was the cause of the restoration, and more than any other sectarian was he persecuted by Charles II.

" He is borne out in all his statements by Mrs. Lucy Hutchinson, that most delightful of women

and of regicidesses.   No doubt the Commons had
a right to punish the weak and perfidious king,
inasmuch as he first appealed to the God of
Battles."

" The present ministry (the Liverpool-Castlereagh
cabinet), although it contains some men of ability,
is supported chiefly by its own weakness, which in
every instance leads or rather compels it to a mean
and abject prostration of the prerogative to the
House of Commons, and by the unpopularity of
the opposition, arising from their having opposed
themselves to the French war and to the grant of
assistance to Spain.   The grand mistake of Mr.
Fox was, that he did not separate the causes of the
war from the consequences, but acted as though,
having espoused the cause of the French revolution,
he must in every instance advocate its measures.
This lost him his party, and swelled the ranks of
Mr. Pitt, a man utterly unfitted for the conduct of
a war, all his plans being based upon, so called,

expediency, and pernicious short-sightedness, which would never allow him to take into his calculation the future."

―――――

" Even the very successes of our naval power contributed, and that in a most influential degree, to form and render extreme the military spirit in France; for, utterly and entirely weaning men from commerce and maritime concerns, they necessarily gave exclusive attention to military affairs, for on the sea, hope, even, did not exist for France."

―――――

" It is not uncommon for 100,000 *operatives* (mark this word, for words *in this sense* are things) to be out of employment at once in the cotton districts (this was in 1820), and, thrown upon parochial relief, are dependent upon hard-hearted taskmasters for food. The Malthusian doctrine would indeed afford a certain means of relief if this were not a two-fold question. If, when you say to a man,

—' You have no claim upon me; you have your
allotted part to perform in the world, so have I. In
a state of nature, indeed, had I food, I should offer
you a share from sympathy, from humanity; but
in this advanced and artificial state of society, I
cannot afford you relief; *you must starve.* You
came into the world when it could not sustain
you.' What would be this man's answer? He
would say,—' You disclaim all connexion with
me; I have no claims upon you? *I can then have
no duties towards you,* and this pistol shall put
me in possession of your wealth. You may leave
a law behind you which shall hang me, but what
man who saw assured starvation before him, ever
feared hanging.' It is this accursed practice of
ever considering *only* what seems *expedient* for the
occasion, disjoined from all principle or enlarged
systems of action, of never listening to the true
and unerring impulses of our better nature, which
has led the colder-hearted men to the study of
political economy, which has turned our Parliament
into a real committee of public safety. In it, is all
power vested; and in a few years we shall either

be governed by an aristocracy, or, what is still more likely, by a contemptible democratical oligarchy of glib economists, compared to which the worst form of aristocracy would be a blessing."

"Commerce has enriched thousands, it has been the cause of the spread of knowledge and of science, but has it added one particle of happiness or of moral improvement? Has it given us a truer insight into our duties, or tended to revive and sustain in us the better feelings of our nature? No! no! when I consider what the consequences have been, when I consider that whole districts of men, who would otherwise have slumbered on in comparatively happy ignorance, are now little less than brutes in their lives, and something worse than brutes in their instincts, I could almost wish that the manufacturing districts were swallowed up as Sodom and Gomorrah."

"Some men—Jeffrey is one—refer taste to palate."

" Absurd terms, when compared, as ' conclusion of a war,' ' conclusion of a peace.'   In the one case it means the end, in the other the beginning."

" I am unable to account for Mr. Locke's popularity; in some degree it may be owing to his having exposed and confuted the absurdities, or rather the absurd part, of the schoolmen.   Hume has carried his premises to their natural and inevitable conclusion."

" The idea of the mind forming images of itself, is as absurd as the belief of Descartes with respect to the external world.   There is nothing in the mind which was not previously in the senses, except the mind itself.   Philosophy, properly so called, began with Pythagoras.   He saw that the mind, in the common sense of the word, was itself a fact, that there was something in the mind not individual; this was the pure reason, *something in which we are, not which is in us.*"

" Socrates seems to have been continually oscillating between the good and the useful."

" To most men, experience is like the stern lights of a ship, which illumine only the track it has passed."

"On William Smith, of Norwich, asking me what I thought of the Monthly Review or Magazine, and of Dr. Aikin, its editor, I was provoked by his evident wish that I should say something in its favour to reply,—' That all men of science or literature could attest that the one was a void Aikin, and the other an aching void.' "

LETTER XIV.

Sunday Evening, Nov. 27, 1820.

MY VERY DEAR FRIEND,

I have been more than usually unwell, with great depression of spirits, loss of appetite, frequent sickness, and a harassing pain in my left knee; and at the same time anxious to preclude, as much as I can, the ill effects of poor J.'s procrastination, —indolence it is not, for he is busy enough in his own way, and rapidly bringing together materials for his future credit as a man of letters and a poet, but shrinking from all things connected with painful associations, and of that morbid temperament, which I too well understand, that renders what would be motives for men in general, narcotics for him, in exact proportion to their strength; and this I could only do by taking on myself as much of the document writing as was contrivable. Besides this, I have latterly felt increasingly anxious to avail myself of every moment that ill health left me, to get forward with my Logic and with my "Assertion of Religion."

Nay, foolish though it be, I cannot prevent my mind from being affected by the alarming state of public affairs, and, as it appears to me, the want of stable principle even in the chiefs of the party that seem to feel aright, yet chirrup like crickets in warmth without light.

The consequence of all this is, that I not only have deferred writing to you, but have played the procrastinator with myself, even in giving attention to your very interesting letter. For minor things your kindness and kind remembrances are so habitual, that my acknowledgments you cannot but take for granted. Mr. Gillman has been ill; Mrs. Gillman—and this leads me to the particular object of this letter—expresses aloud and earnestly what I feel no less, her uneasiness that three weeks have passed, and we have not had the comfort of seeing you. Do come up when you can, with justice to yourself and other connections, for it is a *great* comfort to me; something, I trust, I shall have to show you. A note of warning from one who has been a true but unheard prophet to my countrymen for five-and-twenty years.

May God bless you, my dear friend,

S. T. COLERIDGE.

As I do not intend that these brief notices shall form any consecutive narrative of the events in the life of the writer, any farther than the letters may contain allusions to them, the life itself being, I hope, soon to make its appearance from the pen of his best friend, I shall content myself with the insertion of the following sonnet; it is well worthy a place in future editions. The second sonnet I have found on a detached piece of paper, without note or observation. How it came into my possession I have now forgotten, though I have some faint impression that I wrote it down from dictation, and that it was the transcript of an early, a *very early* sonnet, written pro-

bably at the time when the author's heart, as well
as his head, was with Spinoza.

FAREWELL TO LOVE.

Farewell, sweet Love! yet blame you not my truth;
   More fondly ne'er did mother eye her child
Than I your form: *yours* were my hopes of youth,
   And as *you* shaped my thoughts I sighed or smiled.

While most were wooing wealth, or gaily swerving
   To pleasure's secret haunt, and some apart
Stood strong in pride, self-conscious of deserving,
   To you I gave my whole weak wishing heart.

And when I met the maid that realised
   Your fair creations, and had won her kindness,
Say but for her if aught in earth I prized!
   Your dreams alone I dreamt, and caught your blind-
     ness.

O grief!—but farewell, Love! I will go play me
With thoughts that please me less, and less betray me.

TO NATURE.

It may indeed be phantasy, when I
Essay to draw from all created things
Deep, heartfelt, inward joy that closely clings;
And trace in leaves and flowers that round me lie
Lessons of love and earnest piety.
So let it be; and if the wide world rings
In mock of this belief, it brings
Nor fear, nor grief, nor vain perplexity.
So will I build my altar in the fields,
And the blue sky my fretted dome shall be,
And the sweet fragrance that the wild flower yields,
Shall be the incense I will yield to Thee,
Thee only God! and thou shalt not despise
Even me, the priest of this poor sacrifice.

LETTER XV.

January, 1821.

MY DEAR YOUNG FRIEND,

The only impression left by you on my mind is an increased desire to see you again, and at shorter intervals. Were you my son by nature, I could not hold you dearer, or more earnestly desire to retain you the adopted of whatever within me will remain, when the dross and alloy of infirmity shall have been purged away. I feel the most entire confidence that no prosperous change of my outward circumstances would add to your *faith* in the sincerity of this assurance; still, however, the average of men being what it is, and it being neither possible nor desirable to be fully conscious in our understanding of the habits of thinking and judging in the world around us, and yet to be wholly impassive and unaffected by them in our feelings, it would endear and give a new value to

an honourable competence, that I should be able to
evince the true nature and degree of my esteem
and attachment beyond the suspicion even of the
sordid, and separate from all that is accidental or
adventitious.   But yet the friendship I feel for you
is so genial a warmth, and blends so undistinguish-
ably with my affections, is so perfectly one of the
family in the household of love, that I would not
be otherwise than obliged to you: and God is my
witness, that my wish for an easier and less embar-
rassed lot is *chiefly* (I think I might have said *exclu-*
sively) grounded on the deep conviction, that exposed to a less bleak aspect I should bring forth
flowers and fruits both more abundant and more
worthy of the unexampled kindness of your *faith*
in me.   Interpreting the "wine" and the "ivy
garland" as figures of poetry signifying competence, and the removal of the petty needs of the
body that plug up the pipes of the playing fountain
(and such it is too well known was the intent and
meaning of the hardly used poet), and oh! how
often, when my heart has begun to swell from the
genial warmth of thought, as our northern lakes

from the (so called) bottom winds, when all above and around is stillness and sunshine—how often have I repeated in my own name the sweet stanza of Edmund Spenser :—

" Thou kenst not, Percie, how the rhyme should rage,
    O ! if my temples were bedewed with wine,
    And girt in garlands of wild ivy twine ;
    How I could rear the muse on stately stage,
    And teach her tread aloft in buskin fine
    With queint Bellona in her equipage."

Read what follows as you would a note at the bottom of a page.

" But ah ! Mecænas is ywrapt in clay, and great Augustus long ago is dead."

(This is a natural sigh, and natural too is the reflection that follows.)

" And if that any buds of poesy
    Yet of the old stock 'gin to shoot again,
    'Tis or *self*-lost the worldling's meed to gain,
    And with the rest to breathe its ribauldry,
    Or as it sprung it wither must again ;
    Tom Piper makes them better melody."

But though natural, the complaint is not equally

philosophical, were it only on this account,—that I know of no age in which the same has not been advanced, and with the same grounds. Nay, I retract; there never was a time in which the *complaint* would be so little wise, though perhaps none in which the *fact* is more prominent. Neither philosophy nor poetry ever did, nor as long as they are terms of comparative excellence and contradistinction, ever can be *popular*, nor honoured with the praise and favour of contemporaries. But, on the other hand, there never was a time in which either books, that were *held* for excellent as poetic or philosophic, had so extensive and rapid a sale, or men reputed poets and philosophers of a high rank were so much *looked up* to in society, or so munificently, almost profusely, rewarded. Walter Scott's poems and novels (except only the two wretched abortions, Ivanhoe and the Bride of Ravensmuir, or whatever its name may be) supply both instance and solution of the *present* conditions and components of popularity, viz. to amuse without requiring any effort of thought, and without exciting any deep emotion. The age seems *sore* from excess of stimulation, just as, a day or two after a thorough debauch and long sustained drinking match, a man feels all over like a bruise.   Even to admire otherwise than *on the whole*, and where " I admire " is but a synonym for " I remember I *liked* it very much *when I was reading it*," is too much an effort, would be too disquieting an emotion.   Compare Waverley, Guy Mannering, and Co., with works that had an *immediate run* in the last generation, Tristram Shandy, Roderick Random, Sir Charles Grandison, Clarissa Harlowe, and Tom Jones (all which became popular as soon as published, and therefore instances fairly in point), and you will be convinced that the difference of taste is real, and not any fancy or croaking of my own.

But enough of these generals.   It was my purpose to open myself out to you in detail.   My health, I have reason to believe, is so intimately connected with the state of my spirits, and these again so dependent on my thoughts, prospective and retrospective, that I should not doubt the being favoured with a sufficiency for my noblest undertaking, had I the ease of heart requisite for the necessary abstraction of the thoughts, and such a reprieve from the goading of the immediate exigencies as might make tranquillity possible. But, alas! I know by experience (and the knowledge is not the less because the regret is not unmixed with self-blame, and the consciousness of want of exertion and fortitude), that my health will continue to decline, as long as the pain from reviewing the barrenness of the past is great in an inverse proportion to any rational anticipations of the future. As I now am, however, from five to six hours devoted to actual writing and composition in the day is the utmost that my strength, not to speak of my nervous system, will permit; and the invasions on this portion of my time from applications, often of the most senseless kind, are such and so many as to be almost as ludicrous even to myself as they are vexatious. In less than a week I have not seldom received half-a-dozen packets or parcels, of works printed or manuscript, urgently requesting my candid *judgment*, or my correcting hand. Add to these, letters from lords and ladies, urging me to write reviews

or puffs of heaven-born geniuses, whose whole
merit consists in being ploughmen or shoemakers.
Ditto from actors; entreaties for money, or recom-
mendations to publishers, from ushers out of place,
&c. &c.; and to *me,* who have neither interest,
influence, nor money, and, what is still more
àpropos can neither bring myself to tell smooth
falsehoods nor harsh truths, and, in the struggle,
too often do both in the anxiety to do neither.—I
have already the *written* materials and contents,
requiring only to be put together, from the loose
papers and commonplace or memorandum books,
and needing no other change, whether of omission,
addition, or correction, than the mere act of
arranging, and the opportunity of seeing the
whole collectively bring with them of course,—I.
Characteristics of Shakspeare's Dramatic Works,
with a Critical Review of each Play; together with
a relative and comparative Critique on the kind
and degree of the Merits and Demerits of the
Dramatic Works of Ben Jonson, Beaumont and
Fletcher, and Massinger. The History of the
English Drama; the accidental advantages it

afforded to Shakspeare, without in the least detracting from the perfect originality or proper creation of the Shakspearian Drama; the contradistinction of the latter from the Greek Drama, and its still remaining *uniqueness*, with the causes of this, from the combined influences of Shakspeare himself, as man, poet, philosopher, and finally, by conjunction of all these, dramatic poet; and of the age, events, manners, and state of the English language.   This work, with every art of compression, amounts to three volumes of about five hundred pages each.—II. Philosophical Analysis of the Genius and Works of Dante, Spenser, Milton, Cervantes, and Calderon, with similar, but more compressed, Criticisms on Chaucer, Ariosto, Donne, Rabelais, and others, during the predominance of the Romantic Poetry.   In one large volume.—These two works will, I flatter myself, form a complete code of the principles of judgment and feeling applied to Works of Taste; and not of *Poetry* only, but of Poesy in all its forms, Painting, Statuary, Music, &c. &c.—III. The History of Philosophy considered as a Tendency of the

Human Mind to exhibit the Powers of the Human Reason, to discover by its own Strength the Origin and Laws of Man and the World from Pythagoras to Locke and Condillac. Two volumes. —IV. Letters on the Old and New Testament, and on the Doctrine and Principles held in common by the Fathers and Founders of the Reformation, addressed to a Candidate for Holy Orders; including Advice on the Plan and Subjects of Preaching, proper to a Minister of the Established Church.

To the completion of these four works I have literally nothing more to do than *to transcribe*; but, as I before hinted, from so many scraps and *Sibylline* leaves, including margins of books and blank pages, that, unfortunately, I must be my own scribe, and not done by myself, they will be all but lost; or perhaps (as has been too often the case already) furnish feathers for the caps of others; some for this purpose, and some to plume the arrows of detraction, to be let fly against the luckless bird from whom they had been plucked or moulted.

In addition to these—of my GREAT WORK, to the preparation of which more than twenty years of my life have been devoted, and on which my hopes of extensive and permanent utility,* of fame, in the noblest* sense of the word, mainly rest— that, by which I might,

" As now by thee, by all the good be known,
 When this weak frame lies moulder'd in the grave,
Which self-surviving I might call my own,
 Which Folly cannot mar, nor Hate deprave—
The incense of those powers, which, risen in flame,
Might make me dear to Him from whom they came.

* Turn to Milton's Lycidas, sixth stanza.
" Alas! what boots it with incessant care
 To tend the homely slighted shepherd's trade,
 And strictly meditate the thankless Muse?
 Were it not better done as others use,
 To sport with Amaryllis in the shade,
 Or with the tangles of Neæra's hair?
 Fame is the spur that the clear spirit doth raise
 (That last infirmity of noble mind)
 To scorn delights and live laborious days;
 But the fair guerdon when we hope to find,
 And think to burst out into sudden blaze,
 Comes the blind Fury with the abhorred shears,
 And slits the thin-spun life. But not the praise,
 Phœbus replied, and touched my trembling ears;

Of this work, to which all my other writings
(unless I except my Poems, and these I can ex-
clude in part only) are introductory and preparative; and the result of which (if the premises be,
as I, with the most tranquil assurance, am convinced they are — insubvertible, the deductions
legitimate, and the conclusions commensurate, and
only commensurate, with both), must finally be a
revolution of all that has been called *Philosophy*
or Metaphysics in England and France since the
era of the commencing predominance of the mechanical system at the restoration of our second
Charles, and with this the present fashionable
views, not only of religion, morals, and politics,

> Fame is no plant that grows on mortal soil,
> Nor on the glistering foil
> Set off to the world, nor in broad Rumour lies,
> But lives and spreads aloft by those pure eyes,
> And perfect witness of all-judging Jove;
> As he pronounces lastly in each deed,
> Of so much fame in heav'n expect thy meed."

The sweetest music does not fall sweeter on my ear than
this stanza on both mind and ear, as often as I repeat it
aloud.

but even of the modern physics and physiology. You will not blame the earnestness of my expressions, nor the high importance which I attach to this work: for how, with less noble objects, and less faith in their attainment, could I stand acquitted of folly, and abuse of time, talents, and learning, in a labour of three fourths of my *intellectual* life ? Of this work, something more than a volume has been dictated by me, so as to exist fit for the press, to my friend and enlightened pupil, Mr. Green; and more than as much again would have been evolved and delivered to paper, but that, for the last six or eight months, I have been compelled to break off our weekly meeting, from the necessity of writing (alas! alas! of *attempting* to write) for purposes, and on the subjects of the passing day.—Of my poetic works, I would fain finish the Christabel. Alas! for the proud time when I planned, when I had present to my mind, the materials, as well as the scheme, of the Hymns entitled Spirit, Sun, Earth, Air, Water, Fire, and Man; and the Epic Poem on—what still appears to me the one only fit subject remaining for an Epic Poem—Jerusalem besieged and destroyed by Titus.

And here comes my dear friend; here comes my sorrow and my weakness, my grievance and my confession. Anxious to perform the duties of the day arising out of the wants of the day, these wants, too, presenting themselves in the most painful of all forms,—that of a debt owing to those who will not exact it, and yet need its payment, and the delay, the long (not live-long but *death-long*) behind-hand of my accounts to friends, whose utmost care and frugality on the one side, and industry on the other, the wife's management and the husband's assiduity are put in requisition to make both ends meet, I am at once forbidden to attempt, and too perplexed earnestly to pursue, the *accomplishment* of the works worthy of me, those I mean above enumerated,—even if, savagely as I have been injured by one of the two influensive Reviews, and with more effective enmity undermined by the utter silence or occasional detractive compliments of the other*, I had the probable chance of disposing of them to the booksellers, so as even to liquidate my mere boarding accounts during the time expended in the transcription, arrangement, and proof correction. And yet, on the other hand, my heart and mind are for ever recurring to them. Yes, my conscience forces me to plead guilty. I have only by fits and starts even prayed. I have not prevailed on myself to pray to God in sincerity and entireness for the fortitude that might enable me to resign myself to the abandonment of all my life's best hopes, to say boldly to myself,—" Gifted with powers confessedly above mediocrity, aided by an education, of which, no less from almost unexampled hardships and sufferings than from manifold and peculiar advantages, I have never yet found a parallel, I have devoted myself to a life of unintermitted reading,

* Neither my Literary Life (2 vols.), nor Sibylline Leaves (1 vol.), nor Friend (3 vols.), nor Lay Sermons, nor Zapolya, nor Christabel, have ever been noticed by the Quarterly Review, of which Southey is yet the main support.

thinking, meditating, and observing. I have not
only sacrificed all worldly prospects of wealth and
advancement, but have in my inmost soul stood
aloof from temporary reputation. In consequence
of these toils and this self-dedication, I possess a
calm and clear consciousness, that in many and
most important departments of truth and beauty I
have outstrode my contemporaries, those at least of
highest name; that the number of my printed
works bears witness that I have not been idle, and
the seldom acknowledged, but strictly *proveable*,
effects of my labours appropriated to the immediate welfare of my age in the Morning Post before
and during the peace of Amiens, in the Courier
afterwards, and in the series and various subjects
of my lectures at Bristol and at the Royal and Sur-
rey Institutions, in Fetter-lane, at Willis's Rooms,
and at the Crown and Anchor (add to which the
unlimited freedom of my communications in col-
loquial life), may surely be allowed as evidence
that I have not been useless in my generation.
But, from circumstances, the *main* portion of my
harvest is still on the ground, ripe indeed, and

only waiting, a few for the sickle, but a large part only for the *sheaving,* and carting, and housing, but from all this I must turn away, must let them rot as they lie, and be as though they never had been, for I must go and gather blackberries and earth-nuts, or pick mushrooms and gild oak-apples for the palates and fancies of chance customers. I must abrogate the name of philosopher and poet, and scribble as fast as I can, and with as little thought as I can, for Blackwood's Magazine, or, as I have been employed for the last days, in writing MS. sermons for lazy clergymen, who stipulate that the composition must not be more than respectable, for fear they should be desired to publish the visitation sermon!" This I have not yet had courage to do. My soul sickens and my heart sinks; and thus, oscillating between both, I do neither, neither as it ought to be done, or to any profitable end. If I were to detail only the various, I might say capricious, interruptions that have prevented the finishing of this very scrawl, begun on the very day I received your last kind letter, you would need no other illustrations.

Now I see but one possible plan of rescuing my permanent utility. It is briefly this and plainly. For what we struggle with inwardly, we find at least easiest to *bolt out*, namely,—that of engaging from the circle of those who think respectfully and hope highly of my powers and attainments a yearly sum, for three or four years, adequate to my actual support, with such comforts and decencies of appearance as my health and habits have made necessaries, so that my mind may be unanxious as far as the present time is concerned; that thus I should stand both enabled and pledged to begin with some one work of these above mentioned, and for two-thirds of my whole time to devote myself to this exclusively till finished, to take the chance of its success by the best mode of publication that would involve me in no risk, then to proceed with the next, and so on till the works above mentioned as already in full material existence should be reduced into formal and actual being; while in the remaining third of my time I might go on maturing and completing my great work, and (for if but easy in mind I have no doubt either of the re-awakening power or of the kindling inclination), and my Christabel, and what else the happier hour might inspire—and without inspiration a barrel-organ may be played right deftly; but

" All otherwise the state of *poet* stands ;
　　For lordly want is such a tyrant fell,
　　That where he rules all power he doth expel.
　　The vaunted verse a vacant head demands,
　　Ne wont with crabbed Care the muses dwell :
　　Unwisely weaves who takes two webs IN HAND !"

Now Mr. Green has offered to contribute from 30*l*. to 40*l*. yearly, for three or four years; my young friend and pupil, the son of one of my dearest old friends, 50*l*.; and I think that from 10*l*. to 20*l*. I could rely upon from another. The sum required would be about 200*l*., to be repaid, of course, should the disposal or sale, and as far as the disposal and sale of my writings produced the means.

I have thus placed before you at large, wander-

ingly, as well as diffusely, the statement which I
am inclined to send in a compressed form to a few
of those of whose kind dispositions towards me I
have received assurances,—and to their interest and
influence I must leave it—anxious, however, before
I do this, to learn from you your very very inmost
feeling and judgment as to the previous questions.
Am I entitled, have I earned *a right* to do this?
Can I do it without moral degradation? and, lastly,
can it be done without loss of character in the eyes
of my acquaintance, and of my friends' acquaintance, who may have been informed of the circumstances? That, if attempted at all, it will be
attempted in such a way, and that such persons
only will be spoken to, as will not expose me to
indelicate rebuffs to be afterwards matter of gossip,
I know those, to whom I shall entrust the statement, too well to be much alarmed about.

Pray let me either see or hear from you as soon
as possible; for, indeed and indeed, it is no incon-
siderable accession to the pleasure I anticipate from
disembarrassment, that *you* would have to contemplate in a more gracious form, and in a more

ebullient play of the inward fountain, the mind and manners of,

My dear friend,

Your obliged and very affectionate friend,

S. T. COLERIDGE.

This is one of the most beautiful, the most interesting and, in many respects, the most affecting letter I have preserved; it is a letter which no one but my lamented friend could have written.

I am precluded by the determination with which I set out (not to attach blame to persons farther than blame is attributed by the writer, or to be clearly inferred from the letters or conversations themselves,) from sundry explanations and strictures which constantly occur to me as often as I peruse and re-peruse this letter. The condition here so fully laid open has been in all ages that of the seekers after truth for its own sake; and *exclusively* and NECESSARILY arises from those conditions of mind which render such a course possible. Viewing man, as far as the facts established as *truths,* and the truths which result from antecedent truth enable us to speak on this matter, as subject in all his actions, or rather in the will in which they originate, to external and internal influences which exist antecedent to, and independent of, his will, I cannot hesitate to declare my calm and settled opinion that it is unjust to blame or to praise, or if it *could* be just, only so as applied to the cause, not to the necessary effect. Acting upon these views, it would ill accord with my fixed purpose, if I should blame individuals or systems, or waste time in seeking for proximate or remote causes. All that I have permitted myself is, to narrate, and sometimes to regret results; regrets which to me, and for me, are as *necessary* as the results themselves.

No blame, therefore, do I attach to the parties who permitted such an appeal, from such a man, to strangers. Unworthy as the motives have been termed, by which sundry persons were considered to be influenced, I am *conscious that for them* no other course was *possible*. I cannot call either their motives or their actions evil; it would be untrue if I, with the settled convictions at which I have arrived, were so to characterise them. It will be sufficient for the future that we see what physical suffering and what mental pain were the results. It is only when we apply the experience of the past to the similar or like events of the present, that we add to the sum and amount of permanent pleasurable existence. If a thousandth part of the time consumed in regulating *actions* had been devoted to creating good *motives*, if but a millionth part of the time devoted to the punishment of crime had been bestowed in a right direction, crime, in the form at least in which it now exists, would have been impossible. If the less occupied, instead of busying themselves with spiritual responsibility, respecting which nothing *is or can certainly be* known, had applied themselves to the question of moral and physical responsibility, the lamentable ignorance now prevailing, an ignorance which is synonymous with moral and physical degradation, could not have continued to this hour. If, instead of blaming men for what they are, and are *made to be,* we occupied and interested ourselves with earnest inquiries into the causes of the evils we deplore, with a view to their removal, it cannot be doubted that this real labour of love, if carried on with and through the spirit of love, would in its *very endeavour* include much of the good sought to be obtained. To me it seems that the greatest amount of benefit will result from the labours or the exertions of those, who unite the good to others with that which is—has been made—pleasurable to themselves; from those who seek to make what is genial and joyous to themselves more genial and more joyous to others. This is a labour in which not merely some favourite crotchet, some abstract opinion, or even sincere and honest *convictions* are engaged; it is one in which the best, the purest, the highest sympathies of our nature are enlisted in the service, and in the promotion of those enjoyments, and of those practical occupations from which our own well-being has resulted, or with which it has been associated *.

* As examples of the success attending the removal of the exciting causes of vice or crime, instead of seeking a cure by punishment, I should wish to direct all unprejudiced minds to the results of the system successfully practised by

Much that is now sought to be attained is very pleasant, nay, very desirable, but the means

the celebrated Robert Owen, at New Lanark, founded upon the eternal truth, that men, and, much more, children take their character from the surrounding influences. The result of Mr. Owen's benevolent exertions has proved what can be done with a vicious *population*. The quotation which follows, though not so well known as it deserves, will show what can be effected by a benevolent and decided man with a vicious *adult* population.

"To M. Victor de Tracy.

"*Malwa, 29th March*, 1832.

" During a short stay in Adjmeer, I contrived to visit the Mhairwanah, the former Abruzzi of Rajpootana. It was well worth riding eighty-four miles. I saw a country whose inhabitants, since an immemorial time, had never had any other means of existence but plunder in the adjacent plains, a people of murderers; now changed into a *quiet, industrious and happy* people of shepherds and cultivators. No Rajpoot chiefs, no Mogul emperors, had ever been able to subdue them; fourteen years ago everything was to be done with them, and in seven years the change was effected. I will add, that Major Hall has accomplished this admirable social experiment without taking a single life.

" The very worst characters were secured, confined, or put in irons to work on the roads. Those who had lived long by the sword, without however becoming notorious for their cruelty, were made soldiers; in that capacity they became the keepers of their former associates, and often of their chiefs; and the rest of the population was gained to the by which it is sought are not practicable, the harmonious combinations, to any adequate extent,

plough. Female infanticide was a prevalent practice with the Mhairs, and generally throughout Rajpootana; and now female casualties do not exceed male casualties; a proof that the bloody practice has been abandoned; and scarcely has a man been punished. Major Hall did not punish the offenders; he removed the cause of the crime, and made the crime useless, even injurious to the offender, and it was never more committed

"Major Hall has shown me the corps he raised from these former savages, and I have seen none in India in a higher state of discipline. He was justly proud of his good work, and spared no trouble that I might see it thoroughly. Upwards of a hundred villagers were summoned from the neighbouring hamlets; I conversed with them on their former mode of life, and of their present avocations. Most of these men had shed blood. They told me they knew not any other mode of life: it was a most miserable one by their account; they were naked and starving.

"Now, poor as is the soil of their small valleys, and barren their hills, *every hand being set at work, there is plenty of clothes, of food;* and so sensible are they of the immense benefit conferred by the British government, that willingly they pay to it already 500,000 francs, which they increase every year as the national wealth admits of it.

"Often I had thought that gentle means would prove inadequate to the task of breaking-in populations addicted for ages to a most savage life, such as the Greeks for instance. Yet the Klephts were but lambs compared to the Mhairs, and are not yet possible; and all endeavours to force the time of action have hitherto failed, owing to the time being unpropitious, or to the means being unsuitable; or, still more, from the great, the fatal mistake, a mistake to which benevolent natures are too liable, that of mistaking the changed convictions of the mind for an equally decided and simultaneous change in the habits or actions. From those men the highest good is to be hoped " who have encouraged the sympathetic passions until they have become irresistible habits, and made their duty a necessary part of their self-interest; who derive their most exquisite pleasures from the contemplation of possible perfection, and proportionate pain from the perception of existing *depravation*. Accustomed to regard all the affairs of man as a process, they never hurry and they never pause. Theirs is not that *twilight* of political knowledge

the Mhairs in a few years have become an industrious, a laborious, and well-behaved people.

" I see M. Capo d'Istria has been murdered. I wish Major Hall were his successor, for now I have the greatest confidence in the efficacy of gentle means."

Jacquemont's Letters.

which gives us just light enough to place one foot before the other; as they advance, the scene still opens upon them, and they press right onward with a vast and various landscape of existence around them.   Internal calmness and energy mark all their actions.   Convinced that vice originates not in the man, but in the surrounding circumstances; not in the heart, but in the understanding, they are hopeless concerning no one—to correct a vice or generate a virtuous conduct they pollute not their hands with the scourge of coercion; but by endeavouring to alter the circumstances would remove, or by strengthening the intellect disarm, temptation. These soul-ennobling views bestow the virtues they anticipate.

" That general illumination should precede revolution is a truth as obvious as that the vessel should be cleansed before we fill it with a pure liquor.   But the mode of diffusing it is not discoverable with equal facility.   We certainly should never attempt to make proselytes by appeals to the *selfish* feeling, and consequently should plead *for* the oppressed, not* *to* them. Godwin considers private societies as the sphere of real utility; that (each one illuminating those immediately below him) truth by a gradual descent may at last reach the lowest order. But this is rather plausible than just or practicable. Society, as at present constituted, does not resemble a chain that ascends in a continuity of links; alas! between the parlour and the kitchen, the tap and the coffee-room, there is a gulf that may not be passed. He would appear to me to have adopted the best as well as the most benevolent mode of diffusing truth, who uniting the zeal of the methodist with the views of the philosopher, should be *personally* among the poor, and teach them their *duties* in order that he may render them susceptible of their rights."

The present tendencies are, I believe, adverse to

---

* I consider *both* necessary, nay, desirable. Would pleading for rights withheld have procured their restoration, if also the people had not been aroused by direct appeals to their sense of wrong? Pleading to the oppressed alone would be of terrific danger, did not a sense of justice aided by personal fears create advocates, who end in becoming mediators.

the attainment of any high, pure, or lasting advantage, unless it be from the necessary re-action or recoil. I can conceive of no blasphemy more vile or self-degrading, than that which contemplates the degradation of the moral being into a political or social subjection to combinations, which, if they were as perfect and as practical as they are crude and impossible, would end in solving, by proving, the depravity of human nature.

What is to be said of a science (so called), which tends to the destruction of all that has hitherto been associated with the pure in thought and act, and which has declared, through one of the most favoured and influential of its organs, that it would be of the *highest possible advantage* to Great Britain, if its *country* were wholly destroyed by a volcano, so that its *factories* and *towns* might be compelled to have recourse to other lands for food, and thus sell sundry additional bales of cotton or pigs of iron * ?

* This writer has, in the very article referred to, strangely verified the passage in the preceding letter, in which my excellent friend states that his MS. suggestions have been

Well might Frederic of Prussia say, if it were wished effectually to ruin a province or a kingdom, the surest and swiftest way would be to appoint an economist the administrator. To believe that this most pernicious of all systems can long exist; to think that this faith in mechanics, mental and distributive, could long continue, except as a preparative to something higher or better, or as a condition of a quick and complete re-action, would for me sadden the earth around, and wither the very grass in the fields.

> " Toy-bewitched,
> Made blind by lusts, disherited of soul,
> No common centre Man, no common sire
> Knoweth !   A sordid solitary thing,

made, some to furnish feathers for the caps of others, and some for the purpose of defaming him from whom they were stolen. This writer has done both. He has most grossly defamed the admirable man whom he was incapable of estimating or appreciating, and in the last number of his work has appropriated some of the most striking of Coleridge's views, even to his very illustrations. This writer, formerly a butcher, a man-butcher (I say this *illustratively*, not disparagingly), would be more innocently employed in destroying life than in attempting to mutilate the reputation of the great dead.

'Mid countless brethren with a lonely heart
Through courts and cities the smooth savage roams
Feeling himself, his own low Self, the whole ;
When he by sacred sympathy might make
The whole ONE SELF!   SELF, that no alien knows!
SELF, far diffused as Fancy's wing can travel!
Self, spreading still! Oblivious of its own,
Yet all of all possessing!"

RELIGIOUS MUSINGS, page 90-1.

To you, my dearest children, and to those not less
dear, because equally docile and ingenuous, whom
only, or chiefly, I desire as readers, I would as the
result of my experience say,—cultivate all the social
relations, all the recognised modes of kindly intercourse and intercommunication; yet always preserving, even in moments of the most entire inter-
fusion of mind and the affections, a consciousness
and presence of identity, which alone gives value to
this sympathy and sympathetic union.   So also I
would have you to consider this self as cultivable,
as deriving its chiefest and highest value from its
relation to and dependence upon congenial natures,
which by a natural attraction and harmony are
drawn together, and respond to each other.

To be conscious of existence only, as its sorrows are shared or its pleasures enhanced by affection and love in its *nobler* sense, appears the highest condition of humanity, and this I hold to be attainable. To this I seek to approximate; and this, my dearest friends, every one may to some considerable extent arrive at, who, yearning after the pure and unearthly,

> " Shall, when brought
> Among the tasks of real life, have wrought
> Upon the plan that pleased his *child-like* thought;
> Abides by this resolve, and stops not there,
> But makes his moral being his prime care,
> And therefore does not stoop, nor lie in wait
> For wealth or honours, or for worldly state;
> Whom they must follow, on whose head must fall,
> Like showers of manna, if they come at all.
> His is a soul, whose master-bias leans
> To home-felt pleasures and to gentle scenes;
> Sweet images ! which, wheresoe'er he be,
> *Are at his heart ;* and such fidelity
> It is his darling passion to approve,
> More brave for this—that he has much to love.
> 'Tis, finally, the man who, lifted high,
> Conspicuous object in a nation's eye,

Or left unthought on in obscurity,
Who with a toward or untoward lot,
Prosperous or adverse, *to his wish or not,*
Plays, in the many games of life, *that one*
Where what he most doth value must be won."

LETTER XVI.

Blandford-place, March 1st, 1821.

MY DEAREST FRIEND,

God bless you, and all who are dear and
near to you! but as to your pens, they seem to
have been plucked from the *devil's* pinions, and
slit and shaped by the blunt edge of the broad
sprays of his antlers. Of the ink (*i. e.* your ink-
stand), it would be base to complain. I hate
abusing folks in their *absence.* Do you know, my
dear friend, that, having sundry little snug superstitions of my own, I shrewdly suspect that whim-
sical ware of that sort is connected with the state
and garniture of your paper-staining machinery.—
Is it so? Well, I have seen Murray, and he has

been civil, I may say kind, in his manners. Is this your knock?—Is it you on the stairs?—No. I explained my full purpose to him, namely,—that he should take me and my concerns, past and future, for print and reprint, under his umbrageous foliage, though the original name of his great predecessor in the patronage of genius, who gave the name of Augustan to all happy epochs— Octavius would be more appropriate—and he pro- mises,—*cetera desunt*.

It was about this time that I met with an odd volume of the Tatler, during a forced stay at a remote and obscure inn* in the wilds of Kinder Scout.

* Those who have been kept at a cheerless inn in a dreary country by continued rain in late autumn, without external resource or the means of communication, without books, and even without writing materials,—that is, without paper upon which to write,—need not be told *how delightful*, what an event, it is to meet with a book, such as by a special providence is always discovered in these places when the powers are propitious, such as a stray volume of Sir Charles Grandison, which you will find at the Swan at Brecon, an odd

The book opened at a paper (one of Steele's), giving an account of the writer's meeting with an old friend, recalling to his memory their early intimacy, and the services he had rendered him in his court-ship, the delightful pictures which he calls up of the youthful, animated, and happy lovers, which, with a felicity peculiar to Steele, such was the fineness, the pure gold of *his* nature, he associates, rather than contrasts, with the quiet happiness, the full content and the still devotion (the heart-love),

volume of the Tatler at the inn on Kinder Scout, the fifth volume of Clarissa Harlowe at the inn at Lyndhurst, the Abelard and Heloise, an undomestic translation (which I hasten to recommend to my excellent friend, Charles Cowden Clark, to be immediately expurgated and made *decent*, and *fit* for *introduction* into seminaries, and into demure and orderly families), at the Crab and Lobster, Bonchurch; to Bell's Luther's Table Talk, full of odd things, at Camps Inn, Ilfracombe; the Athenian Oracle, containing many un-noticed contributions by Swift, at the Pelican, Speenhamland; and last, because the most ungenial and most unseemly, Pamela, in one large volume, at the little inn at Bem-bridge Ledge or Point. To enjoy these you must be with-out any other resource, and the book, discovered after a long, and, as you begin to think, hopeless, search, must be one that you have read *very* early in youth, and of which you only retain very faint recollections.

which makes an *Elysium of a home* in other re-spects only *home*-ly.

This picture yet I think one of the most pure and most delightful of that age, for it belongs in its manners and some of its accessories to the past century, I mentioned to Coleridge on my return, and had, as I expected, my pleasure repeated, deepened, and extended. It was a joy and ever new delight to listen to him on any congenial theme, on one congenial to *you* as well as to *him*. I was especially pleased to find that he valued Steele, always my prime favourite, so much above Addison and the other essayists of that day; he denied that Steele was, as he himself said in a pleasantry, " like a distressed prince who calls in a powerful neighbour to his aid, and who, once in possession, became sovereign." Addison was necessary to give variety to the papers, but in no other sense did he give value. Steele's papers are easily distinguished to this day by their pure hu-manity springing from the gentleness, the *kindness* of his heart. He dwelt with much *unction* on the curious and instructive letters of Steele to his wife;

and with much approval on the manliness with which, in the first letters, he addressed the lady to whom he was afterwards united. He quoted the following as models of their kind, and worthy of especial admiration :—

" As I know no reason why difference of sex should make our language to each other differ from the ordinary rules of right reason, I shall use plainness and sincerity in my discourse to you, as much as other lovers do perplexity and rapture. Instead of saying ' I shall die for you,' I profess I should be glad to lead my life with you. You are as beautiful, as witty, as prudent, and as good-humoured as any woman breathing ; but I regard all these excellencies as you will please to direct them for my happiness or misery. With me, Madam, the only lasting motive to love is the hope of its becoming mutual. . . . All great passion makes us dumb ; and the highest happiness, as well as the greatest grief, seizes us too violently to be expressed by words. . . . . To know so much pleasure with so much innocence is, methinks, a satisfaction beyond the present condition of human life ; but the union of minds in pure affection is renewing the first state of man. . . . This is an unusual language to ladies ; but you have a mind above the giddy notions of a sex ensnared by flattery, and misled by a false and short adoration, into a solid and long con-

tempt. Beauty palls in the possession; but I love also
your mind: your soul is as dear to me as my own; and
if the advantage of a liberal education, some knowledge,
and as much contempt of the world, joined with endeavours towards a life of strict virtue and religion, can
qualify me to raise new ideas in a breast so well disposed
as yours is, our days will pass away with joy, and instead
of introducing melancholy prospects of decay, give us
hope of eternal youth in a better life. . . . . Let us go
on to make our regards to each other mutual and un-
changeable; that while the world around us is enchanted
with the false satisfactions of vagrant desire, our persons
may be shrines to each other, sacred to conjugal faith,
unreserved confidence, and heavenly society."

Even when the extreme thrift of his wife—the
necessary result or reaction from the husband's
improvidence—caused him uneasiness, his replies
show the true gentleness of his nature:—

"I assure you, any disturbance between us is the
greatest affliction to me imaginable. You talk of the
judgment of the world; I shall never govern my actions
by it, but by the rules of morality and right reason. I
love you better than the light of my eyes or the life-
blood in my heart; but you are also to understand, that
neither my sight shall be so far enchanted, nor my

affection so much master of me, as to make me forget
our common interest. To attend my business as I
ought, and improve my fortune, it is necessary that
my time and my will should be under no direction but
my own. . . . We must take our portion of life as it
runs without repining. I consider that good nature,
added to that beautiful form God has given you, would
make a happiness too great for human life. . . . You
may think what you please, but I know you have the
best husband in the world in your affectionate

" RICHARD STEELE."

This letter, written about a year after their
marriage, seems to me calculated to appease any
woman who was not both a shrew and a niggard.
Careful attention to fortune, even if it exceed its
fit and just proportion, may, perhaps, be excusable
in a man; in a woman, this most unfeminine and
ungentle property of niggardliness is most unseemly,
even when redeemed, as it was not in this case,
by an upheaped love and devotion to her admirable
husband.

" There are not words to express the tenderness I
have for you. Love is too harsh a term for it; but if
you knew how my heart aches when you speak an un-

kind word to me, and springs with joy when you smile upon me, I am sure you would place your glory rather in preserving my happiness, like a good wife, than tormenting me, like a peevish beauty. Good Prue, write me word you shall be overjoyed at my return to you, and pity the figure I make when I pretend to resist you, by complying with my reasonable demands. . . . It is in no one's power but Prue's to make me constant in a regular course; therefore will not doubt but you will be very good-humoured and a constant feast to your affectionate husband. . . . I send you seven pennyworths of walnuts at five a penny, which is the greatest proof I can give you at present of my being, with my whole heart, yours,

" RICHARD STEELE.

" P. S.   There are but twenty-nine walnuts."

" DEAR, DEAR PRUE,

" Your pretty letter, and so much good nature and kindness, which I received yesterday, is a perfect pleasure to me. . . . I am, dear Prue, a little in drink, but at all times

" Your faithful husband,

" RICHARD STEELE."

" DEAR PRUE,

" If you do not hear from me before three to-morrow afternoon, believe I am too fuddled to observe your orders; but, however, know me to be

" Your most faithful and affectionate

" RICHARD STEELE.

" I am very sick with too much wine last night."

The last passage would, at the present time, be considered evidence of a vicious, degraded course of life, and therefore not confessed to a wife of whom the writer was somewhat in awe. *At that time* drinking was held a mark of good fellowship, and was considered, as indeed it is, far more venial than the vices which at present have usurped its place; vices which partake of the intense selfishness of this age of mechanical activity.

With how sweet a grace does he address Lady Steele, after seven years' intimate communion; and with how much true delicacy does he dwell upon her homely virtues: virtues which, when they attain the great and highest aim of every right-

minded woman, to make home cheerful and happy
to her husband, are, beyond all others, pure and
ennobling; but in this case, that result was neither
sought nor obtained.

" MADAM,

" To have either wealth, wit or beauty, is generally a temptation to a woman to put an unreasonable
value upon herself; but with all these, in a degree which
drew upon you the addresses of men of the amplest fortunes, you bestowed your person where you could have
no expectations but from the gratitude of the receiver,
though you knew he could exert that gratitude in no
other returns but esteem and love. For which must I
first thank you ? for what you have denied yourself, or
for what you have bestowed on me?

" I owe to you, that for my sake you have overlooked
the prospect of living in pomp and plenty, and I have
not been circumspect enough to preserve you from care
and sorrow. I will not dwell upon this particular; you
are so good a wife, that I know you think I rob you of
more than I can give, when I say any thing in your
favour to my own disadvantage.

" Whoever should see or hear you, would think it
were worth leaving all the world for you; while I, habitually possessed of that happiness, have been throwing

away impotent endeavours for the rest of mankind, to the neglect of her for whom any other man, in his senses, would be apt to sacrifice every thing else.

" I know not by what unreasonable prepossession it is, but methinks there must be something austere to give authority to wisdom; and I cannot account for having rallied many seasonable sentiments of yours, but that you are too beautiful to appear judicious.

" One may grow fond, but not wise, from what is said by so lovely a counsellor. Hard fate! that you have been lessened by your perfections, and lost power by your charms!

" That ingenuous spirit in all your behaviour, that familiar grace in your words and actions, has for this seven years only inspired admiration and love; but experience has taught me, the best counsel I ever have received has been pronounced by the fairest and softest lips, and convinced me that I am in you blest with a wise friend, as well as a charming mistress.

" Your mind shall no longer suffer by your person; nor shall your eyes, for the future, dazzle me into a blindness towards your understanding. I rejoice to show my esteem for you; and must do you the justice to say, that there can be no virtue represented in the female world, which I have not known you exert, as far as the opportunities of your fortune have given you leave. Forgive me, that my heart overflows with love and gratitude for daily instances of your prudent economy, the just disposition you make of your little affairs, your cheerfulness in despatch of them, your prudent forbearance of any reflections, that they might have needed less vigilance had you disposed of your fortune suitably; in short, for all the arguments you every day give me of a generous and sincere affection.

" It is impossible for me to look back on many evils and pains which I have suffered since we came together, without a pleasure which is not to be expressed, from the proofs I have had, in those circumstances, of your unwearied goodness. How often has your tenderness removed pain from my sick head! how often anguish from my afflicted heart! With how skilful patience have I known you comply with the vain projects *which pain has suggested, to have an aching limb removed by journeying from one side of a room to another! how often, the next instant, travelled the same ground again,* WITHOUT TELLING *your patient it was to no purpose to change his situation!* If there are such beings as guardian angels, thus are they employed. I will no more believe one of them more good in its inclinations, than I can conceive it more charming in its form, than my wife.

"I will end this without so much as mentioning your little flock, or your own amiable figure at the head of it. That I think them preferable to all other children, I know is the effect of passion and instinct ; that I believe you the best of wives, I know proceeds from experience and reason.

" I am, Madam, your most obliged husband, and most obedient humble servant,

" RICHARD STEELE."

" I sometimes compare my own life with that of Steele (yet oh ! how unlike), led to this from having myself also for a brief time *borne arms*, and written 'private' after my name, or rather another name ; for being at a loss when suddenly asked my name, I answered *Cumberback*, and verily my habits were so little equestrian, that my horse, I doubt not, was of that opinion.   Of Steele, also, it might in one sense, at least, have been said,

' Lingering he raised his latch at eve,
     Though tired in heart and limb !
   He loved no other place, and yet
   Home was no home to him.'

Oh ! the sorrow, the bitterness of that grief which springs from love not participated, or not returned in the spirit in which it is bestowed. Fearful and enduring is that canker-worm of the soul, that

> ' Grief without a pang, void, dark, and drear,
>   A stifled, drowsy, unimpassioned grief,
>   Which finds no natural outlet, no relief
>   In word, or sigh, or tear.'

" I sometimes think I shall write a book on the duties of women, more especially to their husbands. If such a book were *well written*, I cannot doubt but that its results would be most salutary. I am inclined to think that both men and women err in their conduct and demeanour towards each other, quite as much from ignorance and unconsciousness of what is displeasing, as from selfishness or disregard. But to the execution of such a work, or rather such works (for A New Duty of Man is quite as much required, and this must be written by an affectionate and right-minded woman), the present sickly delicacy, the over-delicacy (and therefore essential indelicacy) of the present taste would be opposed. To be of any use it should be a plain treatise, the results of experience, and should be given to all newly married couples by their parents, not in the form of admonition, but rather as containing much important information which *they* can no where else obtain."

LETTER XVII.

Thursday night, May 4th, 1821.

MY DEAR FRIEND,

Mr. and Mrs. Gillman's kind love, and we beg that the good lady's late remembering that (as often the very fullness and vividness of the purpose and intention to do a thing imposes on the mind a sort of counterfeit feeling of quiet, similar to the satisfaction which the having done it would produce) you had not been written to, will not prejudice the present attempt at "better late than never." We have a party *to-morrow*, in which, because we believed it would interest you, you stood included. In addition to a neighbour, Robert Sutton, and ourselves, and Mrs. Gillman's most un-Mrs. Gillmanly sister (but *n. b.* this is a secret to all who are both blind and deaf), there will be the Mathews (Mr. and Mrs.) *at home*, Mathews I mean, and Charles and Mary Lamb.

Of myself the best thing that I can say is that, in the belief of those well qualified to judge, I am not so ill as I fancy myself. Be this as it may,

　　　I am always, my dearest friend,

　　　　　With highest esteem and regard,

　　　　　　　Your affectionate friend,

　　　　　　　　S. T. COLERIDGE.

Of this day and the one following I have a few notes, which appear to me of interest. It must be borne constantly in mind, that much of what is preserved has relation to positions enforced by others, and which Coleridge held to be untenable on the particular grounds urged, not as being untrue in themselves.

———————

" Had Lord Byron possessed perseverance enough to undergo the drudgery of research, and had his theological studies and attainments been at all like mine, he would have been able to unsettle all the evidences of Christianity, upheld as it is at present by simple confutation. Is it possible to assent to the doctrine of redemption as at present promulgated, that the moral death of an *unoffending* being should be a consequence of the transgression of humanity * *and its atonement?* "

" Walter Scott's novels are chargeable with the same faults as Bertram, *et id omne genus*, viz. that of ministering to the depraved appetite for excitement, and, though in a far less degree, creating sympathy for the vicious and infamous, solely because the fiend is *daring*. Not twenty lines of Scott's poetry will ever reach posterity; it has relation to nothing."

---

* Let it always be borne in mind, that this and other expressions in these pages were the opinions which he ever expressed *to me*, and are not to be taken as evidences of doubt generally, but of disbelief in the corruptions of the vulgar Christianity in vogue.

" When I wrote a letter upon the scarcity, it was generally said that it was the production of an immense cornfactor, and a letter was addressed to me under that persuasion, beginning ' Crafty Monopolist.' "

" It is very singular that no *true poet* should have arisen from the lower classes, when it is considered that every peasant who can read knows more of books now than did Æschylus, Sophocles, or Homer; yet if we except Burns, none * such have been."

" Crashaw seems in his poems to have given the first ebullience of his imagination, unshapen into form, or much of, what we now term, sweetness. In the poem, Hope, by way of question and answer, his superiority to Cowley is self-evident. In that on the name of Jesus equally so; but his lines on St. Theresa are the finest.

* In after years he excepted Elliot, the smith, though he held his judgment in very slight estimation.

" Where he does combine richness of thought and diction nothing can excel, as in the lines you so much admire—

‘ Since ’tis not to be had at home,
  She’l travel to a matyrdome.
  No home for her confesses she,
  But where she may a martyr be.
  She’l to the Moores, and trade with them
  For this invalued diadem,
  She offers them her dearest breath
  With Christ’s name in’t, in change for death.
  She’ll bargain with them, and will give
  Them God, and teach them how to live
  In Him, or if they this deny,
  For Him she’ll teach them how to die.
  So shall she leave amongst them sown,
  The Lord’s blood, or, at least, her own.
  Farewell then, all the world—adieu,
  Teresa is no more for you:
  Farewell all pleasures, sports and joys,
  Never till now esteemed toys—
  Farewell whatever dear’st may be,
  Mother’s arms or father’s knee;
  Farewell house, and farewell home,
  She’s for the Moores and martyrdom.’

" These verses were ever present to my mind whilst writing the second part of Christabel; if, indeed, by some subtle process of the mind they did not suggest the first thought of the whole poem.—Poetry, as regards small poets, may be said to be, in a certain sense, conventional in its accidents and in its illustrations; thus Crashaw uses an image:—

'As sugar melts in tea away;

which, although *proper then*, and *true now*, was in bad taste at that time equally with the present. In Shakspeare, in Chaucer there was nothing of this.

" The wonderful faculty which Shakspeare above all other men possessed, or rather the power which possessed him in the highest degree, of anticipating everything, evidently is the result—at least partakes—of meditation, or that mental process which consists in the submitting to the operation of thought every object of feeling, or impulse, or passion observed *out* of it. I would be willing to live only as long as Shakspeare were the mirror to Nature."

" What can be finer in any poet than that beautiful passage in Milton—

———— *Onward he moved*
And thousands of his saints around.

This is grandeur, but it is grandeur without completeness: but he adds—

Far off their coming shone;

which is the highest sublime. There is *total* completeness.

" So I would say that the Saviour praying on the Mountain, the Desert on one hand, the Sea on the other, the City at an immense distance below, was sublime. But I should say of the Saviour looking towards the City, his countenance full of pity, that he was majestic, and of the situation that it was grand.

" When the whole and the parts are seen at once, as mutually producing and explaining each other, as unity in multeity, there results shapeliness— *forma formosa.* Where the perfection of *form* is combined with pleasurableness in the sensations, excited by the matters or substances so formed, there results the beautiful.

" *Corollary*.—Hence colour is eminently subservient to beauty, because it is susceptible of forms, *i. e.* outline, and yet is a sensation. But a rich mass of scarlet clouds, seen without any attention to the *form* of the mass or of the parts, may be a *delightful* but not a beautiful object or colour.

" When there is a deficiency of unity in the line forming the whole (as angularity, for instance), and of number in the plurality or the parts, there arises the formal.

" When the parts are numerous, and impressive, and predominate, so as to prevent or greatly lessen the attention to the whole, there results the grand.

" Where the impression of the whole, i. e. the sense of unity, predominates, so as to abstract the mind from the parts—the majestic.

" Where the parts by their harmony produce an effect of a whole, but there is no seen form of a whole producing or explaining the parts, i. e. when the parts only are seen and distinguished, but the whole is felt—the picturesque.

" Where neither whole nor parts, but unity, as boundless or endless *allness*—the Sublime."

" It often amuses me to hear men impute all their misfortunes to fate, luck, or destiny, whilst their successes or good fortune they ascribe to their own sagacity, cleverness, or penetration. It never occurs to such minds that light and darkness are one and the same, emanating from, and being part of, the same nature."

" The word Nature, from its extreme familiarity, and in some instances, fitness, as well as from the want of a term, or *other* name for God, has caused very much confusion in the thoughts and language of men. Hence a Nature-God, or God-Nature, not God in Nature; just as others, with as little reason, have constructed a natural and sole religion."

" Is it then true, that reason to man is the ultimate

faculty, and that, to convince a *reasonable* man, it is
sufficient to adduce adequate reasons or arguments?
How, if this be so, does it happen that we reject as
insufficient the *reasoning* of a friend in our affliction
for this or that *cause or reason*, yet are comforted
soothed, and reassured, by similar or far less sufficient *reasons*, when urged by a friendly and affectionate woman? It is no answer to say that women
were made *comforters;* that it is the tone, and, in
the instance of man's chief, best comforter, the wife
of his youth, the mother of his children, the one-
ness with himself, which gives value to the consolation; the *reasons* are the same whether urged by
man, woman, or child. It must be, therefore, that
there is something in the will itself, above and
beyond, if not higher than, reason. Besides, is
reason or the reasoning always the same, even
when free from passion, film, or fever? I speak
of the same person. Does he hold the doctrine of
temperance in equal reverence when hungry as
after he is sated? does he at forty retain the same
reason, only extended and developed, as he possessed at four and twenty? Does he not love the

meat in his youth which he cannot endure in his old age? But these are appetites, and therefore no part of him. Is not a man one to-day and another to-morrow? Do not the very ablest and wisest of men attach greater weight at one moment to an argument or a *reason* than they do at another? Is this a want of sound and stable judgment? If so, what then is this perfect reason? for we have shown what it is not."

" It is prettily feigned, that when Plutus is sent from Jupiter, he limps and gets on very slowly at first, but when he comes from Pluto, he runs and is swift of foot. This, rightly taken, is a great sweetener of slow gains. Bacon (alas! the day) seems to have had this in mind when he says, ' seek not proud gains, but such as thou mayst get justly, use soberly, distribute cheerfully, and leave contentedly.' He that is covetous makes too much haste; and the wise man saith of him, ' he cannot be innocent.' "

" I have often been pained by observing in others, and was fully conscious in myself, of a *sympathy* with those of rank and condition in preference to their inferiors, and never discovered the source of this sympathy until one day at Keswick I heard a thatcher's wife crying her heart out for the death of her little child. It was given me all at once to feel, that I sympathised equally with the poor and the rich in all that related to the best part of humanity—the affections; but that, in what relates to fortune, to *mental* misery, struggles, and conflicts, we reserve consolation and sympathy for those who can appreciate its force and value."

———————

" There are many men, especially at the outset of life, who, in their too eager desire for the end, overlook the difficulties in the way; there is another class, who see nothing else. The first class *may* sometimes fail; the latter rarely succeed."

———————

Having been for nearly sixteen years a constant

guest, and, for part of that time, the housemate of
Charles Lamb—the gentle, the pensive Elia—and
his admirable, his every way delightful sister—it
becomes a duty, sacred though painful, to place on
record all that I can convey in a brief space of
the dearest, best loved, and earliest associate of
Coleridge.—Is it too much to hope that the friend
whom he so loved and cherished when young, of
whose splendid talents and their fit application he
always augured so highly, may yet be induced
to furnish what recollections he retains of those
days when Lamb was in the height and vigour of
his genius, relished, and appreciated by troops of
friends, by whom he was loved even more than he
was admired? What names, and what recollections
are there not in those names! Mrs. Inchbald, Mrs.
Barbauld (the two Bald women, as he used to call
them), Lloyd, Hazlitt, Coleridge, Irving, Colonel
Phillips, Admiral Burney, William Godwin, Monkhouse—all dead; Wordsworth, Southey, Sergeant
Talfourd, Basil Montagu, Martin Burney, Mr.
Carey, Barry Cornwall, Robert Jameson, Leigh
Hunt, Manning, Crabb Robinson, Charles Cowden

Clark, Hood, Novello, Liston, Miss Kelly, Mr. Moxon, William Godwin, Mrs. Shelley, Ned Phillips, &c. &c. &c.

I am quite aware that I can convey no notion of what Charles Lamb *was*, hardly even of what he said, as far the greatest part of its value depended upon the manner in which it was said. Even the best of his jokes—and *how good* they were you can never know — depended upon the circumstances, which to narrate would be to overlay and weary the attention.

The following lines of Lloyd will convey some idea, though very imperfect, of this model-man :—

LAMB.

" The child of impulse ever to appear,
  And yet through duty's path strictly to steer!

" Oh Lamb, thou art a mystery to me!
  Thou art so prudent and so mad with wildness,
  Thou art a source of everlasting glee!
  Yet desolation of the very childless
  Has been thy lot! Never in one like thee
  Did I see worth majestic from its wildness;
  So far in thee from being an annoyance,
  E'en to the vicious 'tis a source of joyance."

The first night I ever spent with Lamb was after a day with Coleridge, when we returned by the same stage; and from something I had said or done of an unusual kind, I was asked to pass the night with him and his sister. Thus commenced an intimacy which never knew an hour's interruption to the day of his death.

He asked me what I thought of Coleridge. I spoke as I thought. " You should have seen him twenty years ago," said he, with one of his sweet smiles, " when he was with me at the Cat and Salutation in Newgate Market. *Those were* days (or nights), but they were marked with a white stone. Such were his extraordinary powers, that when it was time for him to go and be married, the landlord entreated his stay, and offered him free quarters if he would only talk."

" I once wrote to Wordsworth to inquire if he was really a Christian. He replied, ' When I am a good man *then* I am a Christian.' "

" I advised Coleridge to alter the lines in Christabel—

  " Sir Leoline, the Baron rich,
   Had a toothless mastiff bitch,"

into—

  " Sir Leoline, the Baron round,
   Had a toothless mastiff hound ;"

but Coleridge, who has no alacrity in altering, changed this first termination to which, but still left in the other bitch."

" Irving once came back to ask me if I could ever get in a word with Coleridge. 'No!' said I, ' I never want.'

" ' Why, perhaps it is better not,' said the parson, and went away, determined how to behave in future."

" I made that joke first (the *Scotch* corner in hell, *fire without brimstone*), though Coleridge somewhat licked it into shape."

" Wordsworth, the *greatest* poet of these times. Still he is not, nor yet is any man, an Ancient Mariner."

———————

" Procter is jealous of his own fame, which he cannot now claim."

———————

" Somerset House, Whitehall Chapel (the old Banquetting Hall), the church at Limehouse, and the new church at Chelsea, with the Bell house at Chelsea College, which always reminded him of Trinity College, Cambridge, were the objects most interesting to him in London. He did not altogether agree with Wordsworth, who thought the view from Harewood-place one of the finest in *old* London; admired more the houses at the Bond-street corner of George-street, which Manning said were built of bricks resembling in colour the great wall of China."

———————

Martin Burney, whilst earnestly explaining the three kinds of acid, was stopped by Lamb's saying,—" The best of all kinds of acid, however, as you know, Martin, is uity—assid-uity."

Lamb then told us a story of that very dirty person, Tom Bish, which I give here for its felicity.

Some one, I think it was Martin, asserted Bish was a name which would not afford a pun. Lamb at once said, I went this morning to see him, and upon coming out of his room, I was asked by a jobber if he was alive? " Yes," said I, " he is B—B—Bish-yet."

Martin defined poetry as the highest truth, which Lamb denied, and, amongst other instances, quoted the Song of Deborah.

The conversation turned one night on the evidence against the queen, especially Majocchi. Lamb said he should like to see them; he would ask them to supper. Mr. Talfourd observed,—

" You would not sit with them?"

" Yes," said Lamb, " I would sit with anything but a hen or a tailor."

A few days before, he had been with Jameson to the Tower, and, in passing by Billingsgate, was witness to a quarrel and fight between two fish-women, one of whom, taking up a knife, cut off her antagonist's thumb. " Ha!" said Lamb, looking about him as if he only just recognised the place, " this is Fair-lop-Fair."

One evening, when Liston was present, and, if I recollect aright, Leigh Hunt and Hazlitt, the conversation turned chiefly on theatres and actors. I have preserved the following recollections:—

Hansard, the printer to the House of Commons, aping the patron, invited Porson to dinner in Lincoln's-Inn-Fields. Everything passed off very well until about eleven o'clock, when the rest of the company departed. Porson alone remained, and proposed to Hansard to furnish two more bottles of wine. One was brought and despatched, when Hansard, having the fear of drunkenness before his eyes, thinking it a sure plan, said his wine was now out, but if Mr. Porson would honour him with his company to-morrow, he should have as much as he liked. This did not suit the Professor, who inquired if there was no brandy?—No! No rum? No hollands?—No! Nothing but small beer. "Well, then," cried the Professor, "we will have a bottle of lightning."

"Indeed, Professor, we have no gin, and it is really too late to get it: it is past one o'clock."

"Past one! *only* one o'clock! Why then I say small beer."

Small beer was brought, and Porson sat till six o'clock drinking small beer out of a wine-glass, taking care to fill Hansard's glass each time, and singing—

> " When wine and gin are gone and spent,
> Then is small beer most excellent."

Liston told us that in crossing Bow-street he saw an old man before him, whom he took for M. Mercier. He tapped him on the shoulder, with—

" Good morning; how are you?"

" What's that to you, you great goose?" said a gruff strange voice.

" I beg your pardon; indeed I *took* you for a Frenchman.

" Did you, by God? Then *take* that for your *mis-take*." And he knocked the poor droll into the kennel.

George Frederick Cooke was once invited by a builder or architect of one of the theatres, Elmerton, as I think. He went, and Elmerton being at a loss whom to invite, pitched upon Brandon, the boxkeeper, to meet him. All went on pretty well until midnight, when George Frederick, getting very drunk, his host began to be tired of his company. George took the hint, and his host lighted him down stairs into the hall, when Cooke, laying hold of both his ears, shouted,—" Have I, George Frederick Cooke, degraded myself by dining with bricklayers to meet boxkeepers?"—tripped up his heels and left him sprawling in darkness.

I retain a very vivid recollection of Manning, though so imperfect in my memory of persons that I should not recollect him at this time. I think few persons had so great a share of Lamb's admiration, for to few did he vouchsafe manifestations of his *very* extraordinary powers. Once, and once only, did I witness an outburst of his *unembodied* spirit, when such was the effect of his more than magnetic, his magic power (learnt was it in Chaldea, or in that sealed continent to which the superhuman knowledge of Zoroaster was conveyed

by Confucius, into which he was the first to pene-
trate with impunity), that we were all rapt and
carried aloft into the seventh heaven.   He seemed
to see and to convey to us clearly (I had almost
said adequately), what was passing in the presence
of the Great Disembodied ONE, rather by an
intuition or the creation of a new sense than by
words.   Verily there are *more things on earth* than
are dreamt of in our philosophy.   I am unwilling
to admit the influence this wonderful man had over
his auditors, as I cannot at all convey an adequate
notion or even image of his extraordinary and very
peculiar powers.   Passing from a state which was
only not of the highest excitement, because the
power was *felt*, not shown, he, by an easy, a
graceful, and, as it seemed at the time, a natural
transition, entered upon the discussion, or, as it
rather seemed, the solution of some of the most
interesting questions connected with the early pursuits of men.   Amongst other matters, the origin
of cooking, which it seems was deemed of sufficient
importance by older, and *therefore* wiser, nations
to form part of their archives.   How this transcript

was obtained, whether from that intuitive knowledge to which allusion has been made, or whether
application was had to the keeper of the state paper
office of the Celestial Empire, I cannot now say. I
can only vouch for the truth of what follows, which,
with the reply to a letter of acknowledgment from
Coleridge, who, having received a roast pig, and
not knowing whence it came, fixed upon Lamb as
the donor, were afterwards fused into an essay,
perhaps the most delightful in our language.

" A child, in the early ages, was left alone by its
mother in a house in which was a pig. A fire took
place; the child escaped, the pig was burned. The child
scratched and pottered amongst the ashes for its pig,
which at last it found. All the provisions being burnt,
the child was very hungry, and not yet having any
artificial aids, such as golden ewers and damask napkins,
began to lick or suck its fingers to free them from e
ashes. A piece of fat adhered to one of his thumbs,
which, being very savoury alike in taste and odour, he
rightly judged to belong to the pig. Liking it much,
he took it to his mother, just then appearing, who also
tasted it, and both agreed that it was better than fruit
or vegetables.

" They rebuilt the house, and the woman, after the

fashion of good wives, who, says the chronicle, are now very scarce, put a pig into it, and was about to set it on fire, when an old man, one whom observation and reflection had made a philosopher, suggested that a pile of wood would do as well. (This must have been the father of economists.) The next pig was killed before it was roasted, and thus—

> " From low beginnings,
> We date our winnings."

Met T. at Lamb's. He seemed to tend towards the negative sensualism. Mentioned Coleridge as one possessed of transcendental benevolence and most exquisite eloquence, as one to whom nations might listen and be proud. He spoke of himself as seared and hopeless, and of Austin, who had, by the force, the clearness, and the originalit of his views and arguments, won him over to the creed of the veritable sceptics, the sneerers, as " the cold-blooded ruffian." Spoke of Macauley, of Moultrie, of Praed. Of Macauley as the most eloquent, of Moultrie as the most pure and high-minded, and of Praed as the most insincere.

Spent a very delightful day at Highgate with Lamb and one or two other congenial spirits. Anster, I think, was one. Had a long stroll over Hampstead Heath; Lamb, with his fine face, taking all the reflective, and the vast volume of the other all the younger and older of the passers-by. It seemed to me—then in my youth and spring of hope and joyance—to realise the olden time; the deep attention with which we all listened, each striving to get nearest to our great teacher, fearing to lose a word, attracted all eyes; many followed us, and still more looked earnestly, as wishing to partake of the intellectual banquet thus open as it were to all comers.

Never will that particular evening be effaced from my recollection. The talk was on duelling, on Kenilworth, and on Peveril of the Peak (which I knew assuredly to have been written by Scott, having myself furnished the first suggestion in a rambling and somewhat excited letter, written amidst the ruins of Castleton, the strong hold of the Peverils), of Sir Thomas Brown, and of old Mandeville. We read old poetry and new; but it

was worthy to have been old.—Lamb observed
when we got home,—" HE sets his mark upon
whatever he reads; it is henceforth sacred. HIS
spirit seems to have breathed upon it; and, if not
for its author, yet for HIS sake we admire it."
Coleridge accused Lamb of having caused the
Sonnet to Lord Stanhope to be re-inserted in the
joint volume published at Bristol. He declared it
was written in ridicule of the exaggerated praises
then bestowed upon the French revolution.

" Not, Stanhope ! with the patriot's doubtful name
I mock thy worth—FRIEND OF THE HUMAN RACE !
Since scorning faction's low and partial aim,
Aloof thou wendest in thy stately pace,
Thyself redeeming from that leprous stain,
NOBILITY; and aye unterrifyed,
Pourest thy Abdiel warnings on the train,
That sit complotting with rebellious pride
'Gainst * her, who from the Almighty's bosom leapt
With whirlwind arm, fierce minister of love !
Wherefore, ere virtue o'er thy tomb hath wept,
Angels shall lead thee to the throne above,
And thou from forth its clouds shalt hear the voice,
Champion of freedom and her God ! rejoice !"

* Gallic liberty.

Sunday. Dined with Lamb alone. A most delightful day of reminiscences. Spoke of Mrs. Inchbald as the only endurable clever woman he had ever known; called them impudent, forward, unfeminine, and unhealthy in their minds. Instanced, amongst many others, Mrs. Barbauld, who was a torment and curse to her husband. " Yet," said Lamb, " Letitia was only just tinted; she was not what the she-dogs now call an intellectual woman." Spoke of Southey most handsomely; indeed he never would allow any one but himself to speak disparagingly of either Coleridge, Wordsworth, or Southey, and with a sort of misgiving of Hazlitt as a wild, mad being. Attributed his secession, to pique that he had not been asked to meet Wordsworth. He had also accused Lamb of not seeing him when with Wordsworth in Holborn. Lamb was much pleased with Wordsworth's attentions, saying, " He gave me more than half the time he was in London, when he is supposed to be with the Lowthers;" and after supper spoke with great feeling of Coleridge, and with a grateful sense of what he had been to him, adding, after a recapitulation of the friends he admired or loved, " But Coleridge is a glorious person," and, with a smile of that peculiar sweetness so entirely his own, " He teaches what is best."

" Miss Lamb, in her very pleasant manner, said, ' Charles, who is Mr. Pitman ?'

" ' Why, he is a clerk in our office.'

" ' But why do you not ask Mr. White and Mr. Field ? I do not like to give up old friends for new ones.'

" ' Pitman has been very civil to me, always asking me to go and see him; and when the smoking club at Don Saltero's was broken up, he offered me all the ornaments and apparatus, which I declined, and *therefore* I asked him here this night. I never could bear to give pain; have I not been called th'-th'-th'-the gentle-hearted Charles when I was young, and shall I now derogate?'"

" Lamb one night wanted to demonstrate, after

the manner of Swift, that the Man-t-chou Tartars were cannibals, and that the Chinese were identical with the Celtes (Sell Teas)."

———————

" He said that he could never impress a Scotchman with any new truth ; that they all required it to be spelled and explained away in old equivalent and familiar words or images. Had spoken to a Scotchman, who sat next to him at a dinner the day before, of a healthy book.

" 'Healthy, sir, healthy did you say ?'

" 'Yes.'

" 'I dinna comprehend.   I have heard of a healthy man and of a healthy morning, but never of a healthy book.' "

———————

" Told a story of John Ballantyne, who going in a chair, the two caddies jostled him a good deal, upon which John remonstrated.   The two caddies set him down, and told him that he being very little and light, was very wrong to choose that mode of conveyance, and argued the matter with him at great length, he being in the chair and unable to release himself."

" One night, when Mathews was going to the theatre at Edinburgh, and was almost too late, he took a coach and ordered the coachman to drive to the theatre. In going up the hill, the horses being tired, the coach made no progress, upon which Mathews remonstrated, saying that he should be too late—he should lose his time. The coachman very coolly said, ' Your honour should reflact that I am losing time as weel's yersel.' "

" On another occasion, when Mathews was returning very late, or, by'r lady, it might be early in the morning, to Edinburgh, his friend, who was somewhat fou, refused to pay the toll, stating that he had paid it before that day. The little girl locked the toll, and he loaded her with abuse, to which she made little reply. After much altercation her mother opened a casement above, and in a sleepy, feeble tone, inquired what the gentleman said. ' Na, mither,' said the child, " it's no the gentleman, it's the wine speaking.' "

" The best pun ever made is that of Swift, who called after a man carrying a hare over his shoulders, ' Is that your own hare or a wig ?' "

Met Mr. and Mrs. Wordsworth, with Mr. Talfourd, Monkhouse, and Robinson. A very delightful evening. Wordsworth almost as good a reader as Coleridge; to a stranger I think he would seem to carry even more authority both in what he read and said. He spoke of Southey and Coleridge with measured respect, and, as I thought, just appreciation. Pointed out some passages in the Curse of Kehama which he admired, and repeated some portions of the Ancient Mariner; also from the River Duddon and the Excursion. Repeated the Highland Girl. He seemed to me to present the idea of a poet in whom the repressive faculty was predominant. Taken altogether, he impressed me very favourably, and I regret deeply that I did not avail myself of subsequent opportunities not seldom proffered by Lamb and Coleridge, of meeting him more frequently. But I then laboured under the impression that he had not acted kindly to that dear and loved being, whom I loved living, and honour dead. Even now, when myself almost indifferent to new associations, I regret this enforced denial of what at that period would have enhanced the value of existence,—communion with that glorious and effulgent mind; but I do not regret the impulses which led to this self-denial.

Met Mrs. Shelley and Mrs. Williams at Lamb's cottage, in Colebrook Row. Was much interested by these two young and lovely women. *Interesting* in every view. Knew Mrs. Shelley from her likeness to a picture by Titian in the Louvre, which is a far greater resemblance to Mrs. Shelley in the beautiful and very peculiar expression of her countenance than would be any portrait taken now. Hers seemed a face, as Hazlitt remarked when he pointed it out to me, that should be kept to acquire likeness. Mrs. Shelley at first sight appeared deficient in feeling, but this cannot be real. She spoke of Shelley without apparent emotion, without regard or a feeling approaching to regret, without pain as without interest, and seemed to contemplate him, as everything else, through the same passionless medium.

Mrs. Shelley expressed much admiration of the personal manner and conversation of Lord Byron, but at the same time admitted that the account in the London Magazine for September was faithful. She censured his conduct towards Leigh Hunt as paltry and unfeeling; spoke very slightly of his studies or reading; thought him very superficial in his opinions; owed everything to his memory, which was almost preternatural. Said that he felt a supreme contempt for all his contemporaries, with the exception of Wordsworth and Coleridge, and he ridiculed and derided even them, and was altogether proud, selfish, and frequently puerile. Mrs. Williams, I think, gave the account of his determining to have a plum pudding on his birth-day, and after giving minute directions so as to prevent the chance of mishap, it was, to the eternal dishonour of the Italian cucina, brought up in a tureen of the substance of soup. Upon this failure in the production he was frequently quizzed, and betrayed all the petulance of a child, and more than a child's curiosity to learn who had reported the circumstance.

" Wordsworth one day said to me, when I had been speaking of Coleridge, praising him in my way, ' Yes, the Coleridges are a clever family.' I replied, ' I know * one that is.' "

* My amiable and kind-hearted friend said here less than the truth, at least as I understand it. Cleverness was not at all a characteristic of Coleridge, whilst it happily suits those to whom Wordsworth alluded, who are or have been clever enough to appropriate their uncle's great reputation to their own advancement, and then to allow him to need assistance from strangers. No one who knows the character or calibre of

LETTER XVIII.

June 23, 1821.

MY DEAREST FRIEND,

Be assured that nothing bearing a nearer resemblance to offence, whether felt or perceived, than a syllogism bears to the colour of the man in the moon's whiskers, ever crossed my brain: not even with that brisk diagonal traverse which Ghosts and Apparitions always choose to surprise us in. I have *indeed* observed *or* fancied, that, for some

mind, whether of the Bishop or the Judge, can doubt, *ceteris paribus*, that the one would still have been a curate and the other a barrister, with but little practice, had they borne the name of Smith—had they wanted the passport of *his* name. It is not always wise to scan too deeply the source of human actions, but I am irresistibly led to the conclusion, that a sort of half-consciousness of " that same " entered into this almost (in one sense *more* than) parricidal neglect. *I blame them not.* I but narrate this as a curious and painful instance how fearfully we are made; how often we prefer our self-will (so termed), nay, even the most sordid injustice, to our duties.

time past, you have been anxious about something, have had something pressing upon your mind, which I wished *out of you*, though not particularly *to have* it out of you. I must explain myself. Say that X. were my dearest Friend, to whom I would be as it were transparent, and have him so to me in all respects that concerned our permanent Being, and likewise in all circumstantial accidents in which we could be of service to each other. Yet there are many things that will press upon us which are our *individualities*, which one man does not feel any tendency in himself to speak of to a man, however dear or valued. X. does not think or wish to think of it when with Y., nor Y. in his turn when with X., and yet still the great law holds good— whatever vexes or depresses ought if possible to be *out* of us. Now I say that I should rejoice if you had a female Friend—a Sister, an Aunt, or a Beloved to whom you could lay yourself open. I should further exult if your *confidante* were *my* Friend too, my Sister or my Wife.

God bless you.

S. T. COLERIDGE.

This letter relates to a domestic, not to say family, perplexity, peculiarly and sacredly my own; one to which no counsel could apply, no consolation mitigate or assuage. Under the circumstances in which I was at that time placed, I could not, I felt it would be premature, to avail myself of the invitation contained in the above letter: and this will, to a great extent, explain much that is contained in the following letters. I had a still farther reason. The individual to whom allusion is made above, was at that time the *ne plus ultra* of my friend's love and fraternal admiration; yet with qualities of head and heart worthy of all acceptance, was partly (almost I had nearly said) on that very account disqualified in my innermost convictions, certainly according to the *judgment* of my then *feelings*, for the office indicated.

LETTER XIX.

Sunday Afternoon, half-past 4.

My dear Friend,

We are quite sure that you would not allow yourself to fancy any rightful ground, cause, or occasion for not coming here, but the wish, the Duty or the propriety of going elsewhere or staying at home. When the Needle of your Thoughts begins to be magnetic, you may be certain that my *Pole* is at that moment attracting you by the spiritual magic of strong wishing for your arrival. N.B. My *Pole* includes in this instance *both the Poles* of Mr. and eke of Mrs. Gillman, i. e. the head and the heart.

But seriously—I am a little anxious—so give my blest sisterly Friend a few lines by return of post—just to let us know that you are and have been well, and that nothing of a painful nature has deprived us of the expected pleasure; a pleasure which, believe me, stands a good many degrees above *moderate* in the cordi or hedonometer of,

Yours most *cordi*ally,

S. T. COLERIDGE.

It must always be borne in mind, that the fragments, letters, and conversations which are here perused at *one* time, were written or spoken at different times, and under the influence of varied feelings and convictions, and the *apparent* discrepancies, or even contradictions, are such as you must be conscious of yourselves as reflective, and *therefore* progressive, beings.

" In the *sense* in which I then spoke and thought, I would again repeat the note to the word PRIEST, originally prefixed to my Juvenile Poems, though perhaps I should somewhat extend it.

" I deem that the teaching the Gospel for hire is wrong, because it gives the teacher an improper bias in favour of particular opinions, on a subject where it is of the last importance that the mind should be perfectly unbiassed. Such is my private opinion:—but I mean not to censure all hired teachers, many among whom I know, and venerate as the best and wisest of men. God forbid that I should think of these when I use the word PRIEST; a name, after which any other term of abhorrence would appear an anti-climax. By a PRIEST I mean a man, who, holding the scourge of power in his right hand, and a Bible translated *by authority* in his left, doth necessarily cause the Bible and the scourge to be associated ideas, and so produces that temper of mind that leads to infidelity; infidelity which, judging of Revelation by the doctrines and practices of Established Churches, *honours God by rejecting Christ.*"

"I have been reading Judge Barrington's Sketches. It is the most pleasant book about Ireland I ever read. I was especially amused by the following

"DIALOGUE BETWEEN TOM FLINTER AND HIS MAN.

"*Tom Flinter.*　Dick! said he;

"*Dick.*　What? said he.

"*Tom Flinter.*　Fetch me my hat, says he,
　　　　　　　For I will go, says he,
　　　　　　　To Timahoe, says he;
　　　　　　　To the fair, says he;
　　　　　　　And buy all that's there, says he.

"*Dick.*　*Pay what you owe,* says he;
　　　　And then you may go, says he,
　　　　To Timahoe, says he;
　　　　To the fair, says he;
　　　　And buy all that's there, says he.

"*Tom Flinter.*　Well, by this and by that, said he,
　　　　　　　Dick! *hang up my hat!* says he."

"Whenever philosophy has taken into its plan religion, it has ended in scepticism; and whenever religion excludes philosophy, or the spirit of free inquiry, it leads to wilful blindness and superstition. Scotus, the first of the schoolmen, held that religion might be above, but could not be adverse to, true philosophy."

" To say that life is the result of organisation, is to say that the builders of a house are its results.

" The 'Friend' is a secret which I have entrusted to the public; and, unlike most secrets, it hath been well kept."

" Interestingness, the best test and characteristic of loveliness."

" Humour is consistent with pathos, whilst wit is not."

" All that is good is in the reason, not in the understanding; which is proved by the malignity of those who lose their reason. When a man is said to be out of his wits, we do not mean that he has lost his reason, but only his understanding, or the power of choosing his means or perceiving their fitness to the end. Don Quixote (and in a less degree, the Pilgrim's Progress) is an excellent example of a man who had lost his wits or understanding, but not his reason."

END OF VOL. I.

LONDON:
BRADBURY AND EVANS, PRINTERS, WHITEFRIARS.

3274288

Made in the USA